The Comprehensive ENFP Survival Guide

The Comprehensive ENFP Survival Guide

HEIDI PRIEBE

Thought Catalog Books

Brooklyn, NY

THOUGHT CATALOG BOOKS

Copyright © 2015 by The Thought & Expression Co.

All rights reserved. Published by Thought Catalog Books, a division of The Thought & Expression Co., Williamsburg, Brooklyn. For general information and submissions: manuscripts@thoughtcatalog.com.

First edition, 2015.
ISBN 978-0692532508
10 9 8 7 6 5 4 3 2 1

Founded in 2010, Thought Catalog is a website and imprint dedicated to your ideas and stories. We publish fiction and non-fiction from emerging and established writers across all genres.

Art direction by Mark Kupasrimonkol
Cover photography by © iStock.com/_Vilor
Cover design by Nick Kinling

To my ESFJ mother for her endless support.

To INFP Hilary, INFJ Heather and ISFP Laura, for the many late night talks about type.

To Thought Catalog, for helping me give ENFPs everywhere a voice.

And to my high school English teacher, who made me take the Myers-Briggs assessment for the very first time.

Contents

Part V. ENFP Relationships

Part VI. How To Make It Work With Every Type

Part VII. Celebrating The ENFP

Foreword

September 24, 2015

She told me, "I truly cannot think of anyone who conveys the wild/restless/passionate ENFP spirit better through their work!" and I thought, *Oh, I am wild, restless, and passionate, am I?* And then I agreed to be a part of this book!

I was first introduced to the Jung Myers Briggs personality typology, back in 2003, when my cousin dropped in from New York to visit me. At the time, my cousin was the Student Body President at Notre Dame University, and already pinned down for future positions by leading companies, such as Citigroup and the CIA. Oh wait; did I just mention the CIA (which is not a company, I know)? Yes, my cousin was in fact invited to become a CIA analyst (I really can't say if he accepted that or not, I just know that he was recruited while at Notre Dame). So, my cousin came over to stay at my condo for a few weeks, and it was during that super fun (but also very contemplative) time we had together, that he introduced the personality test to me. "Take it! It's used by all the leading companies on their employees, it's legit!" he said, then he looked it up for me and made sure I took the most credible one available online, at the time. As it turned out, I was a "Champion Idealist" (also known as ENFP), which garnered a few moments of silence from my cousin, as he sat there, looking at me weirdly. I really can't tell you why he was looking at me like that, because to this day I am still trying to figure that one out, myself!

I continued to take the same test every year, just to monitor any changes in myself. The percentages in my results would vary every year; nevertheless, I would still be a strong ENFP, every single time! The most recent test I took was from a more modern and updated testing facility, where my test results came back as a full-blown ENFP (none of my points of individuality came back below 47 percent)!

What does it mean to be an ENFP, what does it mean to have an ENFP personality type? To me, when I think of what that means, I think of a person born with wings growing out of her heart and roots growing down into the Earth through her feet! Roots and wings— that's an ENFP. We can fly high, but at the same time, we are fiercely grounded in our principles and philosophies that we hold dear in life. Now, I'm not saying that every single ENFP is going to share the same philosophy, the same principle, the same virtues; but what I'm saying, is that whatever those virtues and principles and philosophies may be— you can be sure we've got each our own set of them! Those are our roots. Our wings are the things that nearly drive us to madness, those things that we do which other people would find illogical and maybe even a bit insane! The distance from the Moon to the Earth, is not too far a distance to traverse on behalf of someone we love! Because there is no greater honor than to love and to be loved! So, we'd probably promise the Moon (that would be us flapping our wings); but then you can be sure we'd do everything in our power to make sure that we do in fact fulfill that exact promise (this would be our roots in action). Yeah, we'll promise you the Moon— but we're not going anywhere after we make that promise! We are in fact going to try to steal the Moon for you!

I do believe that there are so many other aspects to an individual other than their personality type, and I don't think that the whole outcome of a person is going to be dictated and pre-formed by their type. I believe that is just one area of our being. But to say that it is a considerable part of our being, would be an understatement. It is a true aspect, not just a considerable one. It may be just one of many aspects; nonetheless; it is a real one.

Heidi thinks I am wild, restless, and passionate... am I? Well, wild to me, means to be like the untouched wildflowers out in the unreachable fields; it doesn't mean being touched all over and being found all over the place in nightclubs and passed out on the streets! Wild, to me, means being unmoved by things like betrayal of trust, discouragements, and really being brave enough to choose the experiences that we allow into our lives. The mighty stag is wild and free— but not just anyone is going to be accepted into his domain! The magnificent eagle is wild and is free— but not just anyone can touch it! So, that's what wild means, to me. And restless... I suppose I am restless in the way that there is an ocean that moves within me! Sometimes, it moves so strongly and so powerfully, that it can toss me around a bit! That's what restless means to me; it doesn't mean not knowing where to go or not knowing what to do! But it is the possession of an internal ocean!

The last thing Heidi said is that I am passionate. What does being passionate mean? Does it mean wanting to hold the world in your hand so that you can bite into it like you would bite into a chunk of chocolate cake? Because if that's what it means, then that's what I am! Does passionate mean you want to walk the streets of the Sun, live there, and say that you are a child of the Sun? Because if that's passion, then I have it! Does passionate mean that it's not alright to just say, "I'm okay," but instead, you've got to feel the need to say, "This is what I dreamt last night" and maybe even, "This is what I dreamt last night, and you were there in my dream, and this is how you felt and I think this is what it means!" Is that what passion means? Because if so, then that's me!

How do we not get tired of all the bursting things that we are? We have laughter spilling out of our pores and tears not yet been born that are ready to surface from our eyes and our ears for so many different reasons— how can we not be tired? Have you ever asked yourself that? Have you ever stood there (or sat there) and asked yourself, "Where did it all begin, and where does it all end? Is there even such a thing as an end? Do endings even exist, are they even real?" I suppose we do get tired, maybe more than others do, but then we also fly higher and we run deeper, and in that light, exhaustion can only be a birthing pain of things so beautiful to come!

I know that being an ENFP isn't going to define my future, my person, and my outcome in life; but I also know that being an ENFP is a pretty damn good thing to be, and it is in this light that I joyfully bring this book into your hands, with full hopes that its positive message will be received and understood, as what was intended for it by the author, during its conception. I welcome you into a greater understanding of yourself, of others like you, and even of those who are not like you whom you will better understand as a result of seeing exactly where you are coming from.

Right now, I am thinking about a circus, and I have no idea why I am thinking of a circus as I pen the very last paragraph for this foreword... maybe it's because it was during those warm Summer evenings back in Florida— at the county fairs and the strawberry festivals, the local circus rides— that I would watch the sun set and the yellow lights turn on along with the street lamps, that I would be met with a sense of wonderment, but at the same time, a heavy feeling born of the desire to have more, to understand more, to go more places! I guess it was in those very places, at twilight, where I would see that I had both wings and roots! I would look up at the rides going around in circles in the sky, and I would realize how far I still had to go! But that didn't mean I thought I couldn't get there! I knew that I just needed to dig a little deeper!

C. JoyBell C. is an author of philosophy of mind, poetry, fiction, and other things wise and wonderful. She has been quoted by Global Leader and Entrepreneurial Innovations Giant, Mosongo Moukwa; Powerhouse Entrepreneur, Speaker and Author, Guy Kawasaki; Dr. Dale Archer, NY Times bestselling Author, Founder/CEO of The Institute for Neuropsychiatry; Chanel rep., Supermodel Cara Delevingne; Demi Lovato; Amanda Seyfried; and many, many more. She is also member of the Editorial Board of the Polish Scientific Journal, Studia Humanitatis Mrongoviensis.

Introduction

First of all, if you are actually beginning this book at the introduction, I fear you may have picked up the wrong book.

Perhaps you were looking for "The Well-Ordered ISTJ Survival Guide," but a ne'er do well ENTP switched the book cover on you as a prank. Or maybe you were on the hunt for, "The ESFJ's Guide To Being Assertive," but bought this book because the store employee recommended it and you didn't want to be impolite.

If neither of these scenarios ring true, I can safely assume that you are an ENFP who has returned to the first page of this book after attempting to read it from the middle and realizing you have no idea what all this "Fi" and "Ne" nonsense is about. In this case, welcome back to the beginning, you over-zealous goof. There are a few things you should know before we get started.

The first thing you should know is that this book won't mimic what you've read about your personality type thus far. Most of the articles that are currently in circulation about type are ceaselessly positive – they highlight the good and brush over the bad. They examine your triumphs and dispel your disappointments. They celebrate your strengths and forgive all of your weaknesses.

This book does not do any of that.

This book is about reality.

This book is about delving into the deepest, murkiest depths of what it means to be an ENFP.

This book is about confronting your bad behaviors. It's about understanding your infuriating inconsistencies. It's about stripping the stereotypes that surround your personality and making peace with who you are at your core.

This book is about becoming the best possible version of yourself.

Through exploring what it means to be an ENFP, I hope you come to understand yourself a little bit better. I hope you find inspiration in the words of other champions. I hope you confront some truths you'd rather keep hidden and rejoice over knowing that you're far from alone. I hope you learn to celebrate your light and find a better way of wrestling with your darkness.

But what I hope, first and foremost, is that by the time you're done with this book, you feel a little more convinced that it's okay to be you – in all your zany, unpredictable glory. Because this book isn't here to tame you. It isn't here to revise you. It isn't here to turn you into an ENFJ, ENTP or INTJ.

This book is here to help you turn up the volume on yourself.

Because if there's anything I'm sure of, it's that the world needs more people like you.

Part 1

Introducing the ENFP

1

Understanding The ENFP

What does it mean to be an ENFP? Chances are, you learned your type via an online questionnaire that was masquerading as the Myers-Briggs Type Indicator®. Maybe your ENFJ boss made you take it as a team builder exercise. Maybe your INTJ partner forced you into it so that he or she could better understand you.

Whatever the case, here's the first thing you need to know about online type assessment quizzes: They only scratch the surface of personality assessment. These quizzes are almost always based on the most elementary type theory – one that pits introverts against extroverts, intuitives against sensors, thinkers against feelers and judgers against perceivers. The truth about type is that none of those categories are mutually exclusive. In fact, you're a little bit of everything.

You're an extrovert *and* an introvert.

You're an intuitive *and* a sensor.

You're a feeler *and* a thinker.

You're a perceiver *and* a judger.

But before we delve into the complications of how you embody each of these preferences while still fitting neatly into the four letter acronym of ENFP, let's do a quick refresher on what each of those terms actually mean.

The Dichotomies

The MBTI® "Letter Dichotomies" refer to the pairs of psychological preferences – represented by letters such as "I" or "E" – that most type tests force you to choose between. The letters and their corresponding explanations are as follows:

E is for Extrovert

Extroverts:

- Gain energy or 'recharge' through social interaction.
- Enjoy having a wide circle of friends and acquaintances.
- Generally feel comfortable in the company of others.
- Are perceived as 'outgoing' or sociable by others.

Vs.

I is for Introvert

Introverts:

- Gain energy or 'recharge' through alone time.
- Prefer to maintain a small circle of close friends.
- Generally feel most comfortable while alone.
- Are perceived as quiet or reserved by others.

N is for iNtuitive
Intuitives:

- Are 'big picture' thinkers.
- Are quick to recognize patterns and make connections between abstract ideas.
- Are more concerned with theories than with concrete facts and observations.
- Focus the majority of their attention on conceptualizing future possibilities.

Vs.

S is for Sensing
Sensors:

- Prefer dealing with the physical world of objects to the intangible world of ideas.
- Are realistic and down-to-earth in their observations.
- Prefer learning facts first and theory second.
- Focus the majority of their attention on either the past or the present moment.

F is for Feeling
Feelers:

- Prefer to make decisions based on how they feel.
- Value interpersonal harmony extremely highly.
- Are naturally in tune with the feelings of others.
- Are more comfortable dealing with feelings than with 'cold, hard facts.'

Vs.

T is for Thinking
Thinkers:

- Prefer to make decisions based on logic.
- Value accuracy over harmony.
- Are not naturally in tune with the feelings of others.
- Feel more comfortable dealing with hard logic and facts than with emotions.

P is for Perceiving
Perceivers:

- Prefer to leave decisions open-ended.
- Work in bursts of energy (often as a deadline approaches).
- Feel trapped inside of strict plans or routines.
- Prefer exploring various possibilities to settling on just one option.

Vs.

J is for Judging
Judgers:

- Enjoy having decisions made.
- Work toward goals steadily and consistently.
- Enjoy following specific plans or routines.
- Prefer settling on one option to exploring various possibilities.

Of course, if all of these categories were mutually exclusive, the world would be in trouble. Introverts would never leave their homes. Extroverts would never leave parties. Intuitives would lack the ability to see, hear, taste and touch the world around them. Sensors would be helpless to form plans or strategize.

The truth about type is that it's significantly more complicated than sorting people into categories such as "Feeler" or "Thinker." Personality type, at its core, is a reflection of how you process information and reach decisions. Sometimes you do this by venturing into the world and gathering new information. Sometimes you do this by withdrawing and analyzing what you have available to you. Each of our brains processes thoughts, feelings and experiences a little differently. And those different methods of gathering and processing information are known as our cognitive functions.

The Cognitive Functions

If you were planning on skimming this chapter in order to reach the more exciting parts of the books, I have some dire news for you.

This is the most important chapter in the book.

You can skip this chapter if you want – I'm not here to clip your wings – but it provides you with the basis for understanding personality type theory on a deep, comprehensive level. The rest of the book is going to be excessively difficult to understand if you do not first understand how cognitive functions work.

So here's my advice for this chapter: Don't skip it. Get up now, take a walk around the block, drink a glass of water, take a nap if you need one, call your mother if you haven't in a while, and then come back to this chapter with a clear mind and a note-taking device.

Because this is about to get complicated.

Cognitive functions were originally theorized by Carl Jung

and written about in greater detail by Isabel Briggs Myers. The "Functions" refer to specific methods of processing information and making decisions, based on your specific personality type. Each type uses four – out of a possible eight – cognitive functions on a regular basis, in a specific order.

The eight cognitive functions are:

Introverted Intuition (Ni)

Extroverted Intuition (Ne)

Introverted Sensing (Si)

Extroverted Sensing (Se)

Introverted Feeling (Fi)

Extroverted Feeling (Fe)

Introverted Thinking (Ti)

Extroverted Thinking (Te)

Whether the function is extroverted or introverted refers to whether it is oriented outward – toward the world of action, or inward, toward the world of introspection. We each use two extroverted functions and two introverted functions. We also each use one intuitive function, one sensing function, one feeling function and one thinking function.

We refer to our intuitive and sensing functions as our perceptive functions, since we use them to perceive the world around us. We refer to our thinking and feeling functions as our judging – or decision-making – functions, as we use them to make decisions.

We all prefer using one of our perceptive functions over the other. The same goes for our judging function. In the case of ENFPs, we use the following functions *in the following order*:

(1) Extroverted Intuition (or Ne)

(2) Introverted Feeling (or Fi)

(3) Extroverted Thinking (or Te)

(4) Introverted Sensing (or Si)

To recap, our perceptive functions are extroverted intuition and introverted sensing. Our judging functions are introverted feeling and extroverted thinking.

We are classified as intuitives in our four-letter acronym because we prefer to look at the 'big picture' (using Ne) *before* taking in the specific details (using Si). In the same vein, we are classified as feelers in our four-letter acronym because we process decisions based on how we feel (using Fi) *before* we consider the logical implications of those decisions (using Te).

We are considered extroverts because we prefer using our main outward-oriented function (Ne) to our main introspective function (Fi). We are considered perceivers because our perceptive function is oriented outward, into the world of action.

This fact that you have a mix of extroverted and introverted functions – as well as a mix of feeling, thinking, intuitive and sensing functions – explains why you often feel introverted when you're processing your emotions but extroverted when you're planning ideas. It explains why you can switch into no-nonsense, get-things-done mode but you also have a soft, deeply compassionate side.

Before delving too far into what it means to use your cognitive functions, let's take a look at exactly what each of them involves.

Extroverted Intuition (Ne)

The ENFP's Dominant (or First) Function

Extroverted intuition (or Ne) is our idea-generating function. It dwells primarily in the future and gains energy through the exploration of abstract ideas and future possibilities. It enjoys brainstorming, speculating and connecting ideas to each other using abstract reasoning.

Ne possesses the unique ability to consider multiple opposing views simultaneously and it does not like to decide firmly upon ideas. It prefers to generate, synthesize and explore them. This function gains the most energy when it is interacting with its external environment – that is, debating ideas with a fellow intuitive type or examining which possibilities exist for the future.

Let's look at Ne in practice.

Ne is the reason why you start ten new projects for every one that you finish.

Ne is the reason why you often contradict yourself in conversation because you genuinely see multiple sides to a situation.

Ne is the reason why conversing with a fellow intuitive makes you feel as though you've had fifteen cups of coffee and an upper.

Ne accounts for your short bursts of innovative energy that peter out as soon as your inspiration wanes.

Ne is the reason why you adore planning for the long-term but can be incredibly impulsive in the short term.

Ne is the reason why you can't properly understand an issue until you've taken the devil's advocate approach to it.

Ne is the reason why your eye always wanders toward better, brighter, more exciting opportunities, even when you're perfectly happy with what you have.

Ne is the reason why you find the beginning of everything fifteen times more exciting than the middle or the end.

Ne is the reason why you never say no to a challenge.

Ne is the tiny thrum of madness in the back of your mind that keeps you constantly moving forward.

Introverted Feeling (Fi)

The ENFP's Auxiliary (or Secondary) Function

Introverted feeling is our primary decision-making function.

Introverted feeling is an analytical function that seeks to discover universal truths about humanity, morality and what it really means to be alive. It looks at everything through a subjective lens and seeks to break down the experience of emotions in order to understand them on a core level.

Introverted feeling can perhaps best be described as an ENFP's digestive system. We take in experiences via our extroverted intuition, then process them and decide how we feel about them using introverted feeling. Fi decides which moral principles we will use to govern our lives and then it fits all new experiences into the framework of those principles.

Until we've taken time to be alone with our feelings, ENFPs have a difficult time making decisions. Fi demands authenticity, which is at the core of every ENFP's value system. We need to know that we are staying true to ourselves in all endeavors – and Fi is the judgment function that determines whether or not we are doing so.

Let's look at Fi in practice.

Fi is the reason why you need to withdraw and reflect on your feelings after a prolonged period of extroversion.

Fi is the reason why you have to assign a deeper meaning to almost everything that happens to you.

Fi is the reason why you experienced such intense mood swings growing up.

Fi is the reason why you spend so much time daydreaming about an ideal version of yourself.

Fi is the reason why you come out swinging when someone says something that goes against your best moral judgment.

Fi is the reason why you feel such intense passion and devotion toward the people and things that you love.

Fi is the reason why you've considered whether or not you're an introvert at some point in your life.

Fi is the reason why you've probably felt misunderstood for the majority of your life.

Extroverted Thinking (Te)

The ENFP's Tertiary (or Third) Function

Extroverted thinking is our secondary decision-making function. Extroverted thinking is introverted feelings executive assistant, if you will, and it works to back up introverted feeling in whatever decisions it comes to.

Extroverted thinking – as an isolated function – is all about imposing order on its external environment. It looks at everything through a results-based lens and is incredibly efficient at executing plans that yield tangible, beneficial results. Extroverted thinking takes a top-down approach to almost everything – it looks at where it wants to be and then works backwards to figure out how to get there. It has its end goal in mind at all times and tends to believe that the end almost always justify the means.

Te is an extroverted function that is skilled at constructing arguments in a logical, indisputable fashion. It is difficult to argue with a Te user because they get right to the point and relate everything back to usefulness – if an idea or a detail does not support a meaningful end, then the extroverted thinker has no interest in it. They argue from the position of what is indisputably logical and immediately apparent – this is why ENFPs are often skilled debaters, despite being introverted feelers at their core.

17

Let's look at Te in practice.

Te is the reason why you are good at accomplishing your goals, even if they are driven by pure emotion.

Te is the reason why you argue with cold, detached logic when you're angry or worked up.

Te is the reason why you have a hard time motivating yourself to do basically anything that you can't see the immediate benefit of.

Te is the reason why you are surprisingly resourceful when you want something.

Te is the reason why you're good at phrasing things in a way that people have a difficult time arguing with.

Te is the reason why you can sometimes convincingly fake that you're in touch with the world outside of your own mind.

Introverted Sensing (Si)

The ENFP's Inferior (or Last) Function

Introverted sensing is the last function in the ENFP's stack – also known as our inferior function. It's important to note here that the traditional definition of introverted sensing does not necessarily relate to the ENFP's experience of it. Because it is our repressed function, it often manifests itself in unhealthy or counterproductive ways.

As an isolated function, Si is focused on routine, tradition and integrating past experiences into the present. It places a high level of trust in authority, institutions and societal norms. Si is highly detail-oriented and is skilled at remembering specific pieces of information. Si users tend to have excellent memories and use their past experiences to plan for the future – they chronically assume that the future will resemble the past.

Doesn't sound like you? That's because inferior or repressed Si manifests itself through rebellion.

Let's look at Si in practice for the ENFP's.

Underdeveloped Si is the reason why you are impatient with social norms or pleasantries and feel resentment towards 'The man.'

Underdeveloped Si is the reason why you don't want to lead a traditional life.

Underdeveloped Si is the reason why you often forget to eat, sleep or bathe when you are engrossed in a new project or endeavor.

Underdeveloped Si is the reason why your anxiety may manifest itself physically.

Underdeveloped Si is the reason why you distrust authority and traditional methods of getting things done.

Healthy Si is the reason why you are able to follow through on your goals and projects even once they've grown boring.

Healthy Si is the reason why you don't repeat your big mistakes.

Healthy Si is the reason why you make a deliberate effort to take care of yourself physically and emotionally.

Healthy Si is the reason why you're comforted by past

experiences and use them as a reassurance that if things worked out for you before, they can work out again.

Si is the reason why you're prone to intense bouts of sentimentality.

Si is the reason why you're still alive.

2

How The Functions Manifest

Let's take a look at how we perceive our own functions.

Think of it like this: You are in a swimming pool and your first or "dominant" function (in the ENFP's case, extroverted intuition) is the water. It's everywhere. It's what you do without thinking about it. It's your natural first impulse to every situation – it comes to you so naturally that you may not even notice yourself using it.

Introverted feeling (known as your auxiliary function) is like the ladder, or the waterslide. To an extent, you can choose to use it or not use it. You are very aware of its presence. You can't make it go away, but you can temporarily ignore it. You have to swim through the water to get there.

Your third and fourth functions – or your "tertiary" and "inferior" functions (extroverted thinking and introverted sensing for the ENFP) – are less accessible to you, as you may not fully develop them until you are nearing middle age. When you're younger, your tertiary and inferior functions are primarily called upon when you are under stress. If you started drowning in the water, your tertiary and inferior functions would be the life raft that you cling to. Eventually, you can integrate them to become pool toys that you use on a regular basis. Once you've done this, you will finally have a well-balanced, relaxing pool experience. We can also refer to this as type actualization.

Your cognitive functions develop in chronological order, as you age. In the following chapters we will take a look at when each function begins to mature and take on a more significant role in the ENFP's brain. In the meantime, however, it's important to examine the unique relationships our functions have with each other.

Function Pairs

Though extroverted intuition and introverted feeling are the most dominant functions in the ENFP's brain, they are surprisingly independent of one another. Think of extroverted intuition and introverted feeling as a married couple – they interact a great deal and have learned to complement one another, but there is no inherent blood relationship between them.

Where there is a close, mutual relation is between the two perceptive functions and the two judging functions. Introverted sensing is like extroverted intuition's biological child and extroverted thinking is like introverted feeling's biological child. Everything extroverted intuition does affects and is noticed by introverted sensing. Everything introverted feeling does affects and is noticed by extroverted thinking.

While extroverted intuition is out in the world, discussing ideas and theorizing future plans, introverted sensing is tagging along in the background, making notes and keeping track of extroverted intuition's perceptions.

While introverted feeling is sitting indoors processing the ENFP's experiences, extroverted thinking is taking note of introverted feeling's decisions and theorizing ways in which they could be implemented.

Eventually, Te and Si will mature and push back against their parent functions. Si might tell Ne, "You tried this before and it didn't work." Te might tell Fi, "This decision is impractical and we ought to look at more logical options." Other times, Si and Te will subtly manipulate their parents into making the decisions *they* want, without their parents noticing or resisting.

The maturation of their tertiary and inferior functions will allow the ENFP to become a well-rounded individual. But at the end of the day, extroverted intuition and introverted feeling will always be the main functions in charge of the ENFP's brain – and they will consequently always be the functions that you end up trusting the most.

So What Does It Mean To Be An ENFP?

Now that you know a bit about how your brain takes in information and makes decisions, how does this manifest in the real world?

On the surface, ENFPs appear to be bubbly, confident, personable and enthusiastic. They are fiercely engaging personalities who care passionately about the world that surrounds them and the people who make it up. They have a particular knack for riling people up and making those around them feel comfortable, appreciated and loved.

What is less apparent about the ENFP is the rich inner world that exists beneath their surface. ENFPs feel and experience life on an incredibly deep level – they are constantly picking apart new experiences to decipher their meaning and determine their significance. This type may seem wildly extroverted to others, but they often feel the most in touch with themselves when they are alone. Their solitary world is where the ENFP goes to make sense of the lives they are living and process what their experiences truly mean.

Though they are agreeable on the surface, ENFPs are often extremely driven individuals. This type is compelled by a strong set of ideals that they often conceive at an incredibly young age. They may jump between careers, opportunities and experiences in their adult lives but nonetheless feel as though they're perfectly on track to becoming the kind of person they want to be. For the ENFP, experiences are not ends in themselves but vessels through which they can uncover deeper, more complex truths about life. Therefore, the more experiences they draw in and process in a meaningful way, the more fulfilled the ENFP feels.

Of course, this type is not without its struggles. In their younger years, ENFPs may lack the follow-through they require to get the most out of their experiences. They may give up on new projects prematurely or find themselves constantly getting distracted by more exciting options and engaging in a never-ending chase for the next great 'high.' This tendency is likely to even out as they age, but an ENFP who does not learn to apply judgment to their perceptions is at risk of wandering between experiences indefinitely – ultimately leaving them feeling unfulfilled.

At their best, ENFPs are passionate, creative, enthusiastic, driven and genuinely inspirational to those around them. This type possesses a unique mixture of emotional intelligence, critical thinking skills and pure mental strength which, when combined, will get them to just about wherever they'd like to be in life.

Frequently Asked Questions About ENFPs

Can my personality type change?

The short answer is no.

The long answer is also no.

If you are using an online test to assess your personality type, it is highly likely that you will test as various different types over the course of your life. This is because most online tests are based on the four-letter dichotomies and not the cognitive functions. This makes the test results highly subjective and prone to variance based on where one is in the development of their cognitive functions.

Throughout this book, the development of the ENFP's dominant, auxiliary, tertiary and inferior cognitive functions will be explored at great length. You will come to understand how your personality presents itself at different stages of your lifespan, and across various stressful situations. Which personality *tools* you use to interact with the world will depend on where you are in terms of cognitive development as well as which external circumstances you are facing. However, your personality type itself is pervasive across the lifespan.

If I'm an ENFP, why do I feel like an introvert?

ENFPs are known as the 'most introverted extroverts' and mistake themselves for introverts in high frequency.

The reason for this is that our dominant extroverted function – extroverted intuition – is significantly more concerned with the external world of possibilities and ideas than it is with the external world of people. We gain energy from brainstorming, theorizing, debating and imagining new possibilities for the future. If this can be done aloud, in the company of likeminded people, we gain maximum energy. If no such people are available, we'll simply brainstorm, theorize and imagine new possibilities on our own. Either way we are activating our extroverted intuition. Ironically, we can use our dominant extroverted function either alone or around others. It is, in many senses, an ambiverted function.

The other reason ENFPs identify highly with introversion is that we require a significant amount of alone time to process new experiences via our auxiliary introverted feeling. ENFPs place a high value on authenticity and we must constantly 'check in' with ourselves to ensure that we are living life in accordance with our internal system of morals and ideals. This causes us to require significantly more alone time than almost any other extroverted type.

How do I figure out if I'm an INFP or an ENFP?

INFPs and ENFPs use all the same cognitive functions, but in a slightly different order. INFPs use introverted feeling first, extroverted intuition second, introverted sensing third and extroverted thinking fourth. A few methods of differentiating between the ENFP and the INFP personality type are as follows:

For INFPs, feelings precede actions. They need to determine how they feel about a given situation before jumping into it and have a very difficult time acting on anything if they do not *first* feel passionately about it.

For ENFPs, actions precede feelings. They tend to jump into new situations enthusiastically, as soon as a new idea occurs to them, and then withdraw to process their feelings about the situation *after* having acted on it.

Another method of discerning whether you are an ENFP or an INFP is to determine which function you are less comfortable with: Extroverted thinking or introverted sensing.

The ENFP's inferior function is introverted sensing. This often gives them a "screw the system" mentality and motivates them to seek unconventional methods of going about almost everything. Their tertiary function is extroverted thinking, which means they are often highly resourceful and tend to be adept (though not necessarily preemptive) at solving problems in their external environment. "Where there's a will, there's a way," is basically the ENFP motto.

The INFP's inferior function is extroverted thinking. This often gives them an, "Individuality above all else" mentality that prevents them from engaging in any action that is not in line with their personal values. Their tertiary function is introverted sensing, which means they are better than ENFPs at remembering facts, have a higher attention to detail and may take more interest in the history or tradition behind their interests (i.e. an INFP is more likely to learn everything about their favorite musical artist than an ENFP, who is more likely to only listen to the songs he or she likes).

At the end of the day, the only true way to discern your personality type is to learn about the cognitive functions as thoroughly as possible and determine which ones you use most regularly and in which order.

Common Misconceptions About ENFPs

As with any personality system, certain stereotypes are bound to develop. This is particularly true for the ambiverted ENFP – what they reveal to others is often quite different from the way in which they truly experience the world. Here are a few common stereotypes associated with the ENFP personality type and the realities that correspond to them.

Perception: ENFPs are incredibly laid back

Reality: ENFPs are selectively laid-back. They're big-picture thinkers, which means that small, everyday concerns don't always make the radar. But when it comes to their goals and desires, ENFPs are the least chill people imaginable. This type is constantly at work analyzing, evaluating and making connections between everything that happens around them. ENFPs may have messy houses but they have clear visions of the future and they don't let anything get in the way of what they really want.

Perception: ENFPs wear their hearts on their sleeve

Reality: ENFPs are warm. They're welcoming. They're kind. But what they are not is comfortable with personal disclosure. This type uses extroverted intuition and extroverted thinking to interact with the world around them, which means they're much more comfortable asking questions and debating ideas than they are proclaiming their feelings. Unless you're a particularly close friend, anything you know about the ENFP's inner world is probably just the peak of the iceberg.

Perception: ENFPs are commitment-phobes

Reality: ENFPs are not always quick to jump into serious relationships but this is more often an issue of compatibility than one of commitment. ENFPs connect relatively quickly with most people. But they want more than a surface-level connection and a few common interests: they are searching for a specific, intense relationship that both challenges and grows them. If they find this, they are all in. If not, the horizons are still being scanned for what else is out there.

Perception: ENFPs are always happy

Reality: ENFPs hold the pervasive belief that there is always something left to look forward to. This does not at all translate to constant happiness. Though this type gives off a light-hearted, fun-loving air, they actually take life quite seriously. ENFPs feel their lows just as intensely as they feel their highs – they just aren't as comfortable expressing negative emotions as they are positive ones.

Perception: ENFPs are social butterflies

Reality: ENFPs love people – that's no secret. What's not as obvious is that ENFPs put an incredible amount of stock into their personal relationships. Trying to maintain five hundred surface level friendships would be exhausting for this type. They give off a friendly air, but are really unable to maintain more than a handful of close relationships at a time.

Perception: ENFPs are the ultimate free spirits

Reality: ENFPs are not the free-spirited hippy types that they are so often made out to be. Though their values are liberal and their methods unconventional, ENFPs are incredibly driven folk who almost always have a clear-cut goal in mind.

They don't want to go wherever the wind blows them – they want to embody the storm. And they'll take down whatever stands in their way.

3

ENFPs And The Enneagram

The ENFP personality type is not mutually exclusive with other personality inventories. Just as we can use our four-letter type as a method of narrowing down our personalities and understanding more about ourselves, we can also combine that knowledge with other personality inventories in order to understand differences that exist within specific types.

One personality inventory that combines particularly nicely with the ENFP personality is known as the Enneagram of Personality. This inventory presents nine different types (labeled types One through Nine) and each number represents a collection of basic fears and motivations that drive that particular type (Riso & Hudson, 1997).

While the research correlating Myers-Briggs test results with the Enneagram test results is still in its infancy, most ENFPs claim to identify with either Enneagram Type 7 (The Enthusiast), Type 4 (The Individualist) or Type 2 (The Helpers).

In order to delve deeper into the basic motivations of different ENFPs, the following chapter will examine the top three most common ENFP Enneagram types. Most ENFPs will find themselves relating to all three types in some regard, but will likely relate best or most fully to one.

Type 2 ENFPs: The Helpers

Type 2 ENFPs are all about pursuing their vision of a kinder world. These ENFPs are particularly in touch with their introverted feeling and may be more comfortable expressing their emotions than their Type 7 or Type 4 counterparts. They place their loved ones at the center of their world and are incredibly nurturing of their personal relationships.

This type may come across as warmer and bubblier than other ENFPs. They are the ultimate people-pleasers who will go out of their way to ensure that nobody thinks ill of them. They are often highly invested in their community and tend to channel their extroverted intuition towards visions of a more understanding world, where kindness and connection prevail. They are deeply empathetic towards others and display openness and vulnerability in their own lives, hoping to inspire others to feel comfortable doing the same.

At their best, type 2 ENFPs are generous, selfless, compassionate and understanding.

At their worst, they are blameful, demanding, self-pitying and desperate for attention.

As with any ENFP, Type 2s require a significant amount of external validation – they need regular reminders from others that they're good people who are worthy of love. As a result, this type may struggle to apply extroverted thinking to their judgments because introverted feeling is set on achieving validation from others at all costs. More so than other ENFP types, type 2s are likely to compromise their own desires in order to please others and receive positive validation.

In an unhealthy state, Type 2 ENFPs project blame externally. They place fault on others for behaving immorally, being unappreciative of the ENFP and lacking compassion for others. *It is of the utmost importance that the Type 2 ENFP continues to perceive himself or herself as a good and principled individual* – they will cling to this belief about themselves at all costs. In a negative spiral, this type may be prone to bouts of intense hypochondria, as a subconscious means of gleaning attention from others and forcing their loved ones to nurture and take care of them, the way the ENFP feels they deserve to be taken care of.

The Type 2 ENFP's route to personal growth is through their extroverted thinking. By learning to temporarily detach from their need for validation, this type will steadily become more assertive, independent and – ironically – more principled.

Type 4 ENFPs: The Artists

Type 4 ENFPs are all about dwelling in the deep end of their thoughts, feelings and personal truths. This type is particularly focused on authenticity and may be slightly more introverted than their Type 7 or Type 2 counterparts. They enjoy exploring the rich inner world of their introverted feeling and may use extroverted intuition as somewhat of a muse – using it to pull in new experiences to analyze and dissect.

This type may come across as more tortured or conflicted than the average ENFP. They can be quite serious in nature and they long for profound connections with deep, intellectual personalities. They are particularly attracted to other artistic individuals – musicians, poets, painters, writers and other creative types, whom they often feel are the only people capable of truly understanding them. Type 4 ENFPs relish in creative expression and have little interest in conforming to societal norms – their authenticity is of the utmost importance to them.

At their best, type 4 ENFPs are highly complex, creative, intelligent and in touch with their deepest thoughts and emotions.

At their worst, they are spiteful, jealous, insecure and emotionally masochistic.

The type 4 ENFP's deepest fear is being average or insignificant. They wish to give back to the world through the gift of their rich creativity and they feel an intense need to have their true voice be heard. This type is usually incredibly artistically inclined and they bring their unique worldview to light through their art form of choice. They are the ultimate outside-the-box artists who charm and entice their audiences with wildly unique performances or products.

In an unhealthy state, Type 4 ENFPs fall victim to the 'Special Snowflake Syndrome.' They feel the need to prove that they are deeper and more unique than those around them and they may subtly put down others for exhibiting commonplace or average behavior. They will go searching for external validation that they are interesting, authentic and deep and may lash out at others for failing to understand them.

The Type 4 ENFP's route to personal growth is through their extroverted thinking. This type grows through the realization that the world is not entirely subjective and that a degree of objective judgment can be applied to their thoughts and emotions – helping to keep them grounded in the physical world that surrounds them.

Type 7 ENFPs: The Adventurers

Type 7 ENFPs are all about pursuing the next great adventure. These ENFPs are particularly focused on their extroverted intuition and may spend slightly more time engaged in the external realm of ideas and adventures than their type 4 and type 2 counterparts. They are fiercely fascinated by whatever it is that engages them in the moment and will explore new interests with an unrelenting vigor.

These types may come across as slightly more aggressive than the average ENFP. They maintain a clear vision of what they want at all times, and are not afraid to step on a few toes to get it. They are kind and caring, but may not show you their soft side until you get to know them well, or until you require some sort of help from them.

At their best, Type 7 ENFPs are bold, adventurous, decisive and capable.

At their worst, they are avoidant, irresponsible, self-destructive and particularly prone to addiction.

Type 7s turn to the outer world of adventures and opportunities to deal with internal problems. As a result, they may lose sync with their introverted feeling while under stress and be particularly prone to falling into dominant-tertiary loops (an unhealthy mental state in which the ENFP moves directly from their extroverted intuition to their extroverted thinking, without consulting their introverted feeling in between).

The ENFP Type 7's fatal flaw is escapism. This type may be particularly prone to flakey behavior as they move quickly between jobs, relationships and situations that do not suit them. They dislike dwelling in negative emotions and avoid them at absolutely all costs. This type of ENFP may have been raised in an environment where emotional expression was not appreciated or encouraged. They experience extreme difficulty processing negative emotions and may be particularly prone to physical manifestations of anxiety or stress.

The Type 7 ENFP's route to personal growth is through their introverted feeling. In order to become a more stable individual, Type 7 ENFPs need to learn to fully process their emotions and decide what they think or feel about a given situation before jumping into action.

Applying The Enneagram

For more information on the Enneagram of Personality, visit The Enneagram Institute Homepage at https://www.enneagraminstitute.com/.

4

25 Struggles Only ENFPs Will Understand

ENFPs come in all shapes and sizes. Some of us are expressive and some of us are reserved. Some of us are adventurous and some of us are cautious. Some of us are Enneagram Types 2, 4 and 7 and some of us are Enneagram types 8, 3 and 9. But regardless of which behaviors we embody on the outside, there are a few joys and challenges that all of us inherently share.

1. Getting your energy from social interaction, but disliking superficial conversations. Yes, I want to go to a party tonight. But a party full of contemplative people who want to alternate between taking shots and discussing the meaning of life.

2. Being very socially conscious but also fiercely individualistic. This means always wanting to fit in with a group, but never wanting to compromise your personality to do so.

3. The constant tug-of-war between 'YES, I WANT TO GO EXPERIENCE EVERYTHING RIGHT NOW' and 'Wow, I

need a lot of time to process these experiences, can I take a breather?'

4. Having a thousand great ideas that you never follow through on.

5. Regularly forgetting that your physical needs exist.

6. Getting into the perfect job/relationship/groove and hearing that nagging voice in the back of your mind going "But maybe there's something even BETTER out there…"

7. Constantly contradicting yourself because you genuinely see multiple sides to most situations.

8. Everyone thinking you're flirting with them, all of the time.

9. Being a HUGE, UNSTOPPABLE FORCE of creativity and productivity… an hour before the deadline.

10. Getting bored 500 times faster than the average human being.

11. Constantly biting off more than you can chew… and then chewing it out of stubbornness.

12. Stressing out friends and acquaintances who don't like straying from the original plan.

13. Working towards a constantly altering notion of your "ideal self."

14. When you have to complete a task that you simply cannot find a way to make fun.

15. Begrudgingly identifying Peter Pan as your spirit animal.

16. People underestimating your intelligence because you lead with the fun, upbeat parts of your personality.

17. Needing significantly more alone time than other extraverts.

18. Others being surprised that you hold such strong opinions and beliefs, despite your easy-going nature.

19. Trying to explain to the people closest to you that yes, you love pretty much everyone, but you love them the MOST.

20. People thinking you're looking for advice when you simply need to process things out loud.

21. Staying in bad relationships because you focus on how things COULD be rather than how they are.

22. Wanting to be alone... but like, with other people nearby.

23. Appearing shallow because of your tendency to flit from topic to topic in conversation, with lightning speed.

24. Having a fiercely independent streak... but getting bored without company.

25. Being a walking contradiction in almost every way, but knowing that you wouldn't change a thing, even if you could.

Part 2

Growing Up ENFP

5

ENFPs Across The Lifespan

*"It takes courage to grow up and become
who you really are."*
–E.E. Cummings

Being an ENFP is a life sentence.

Though personality type is theorized to not solidify until one's teen years, ENFPs often begin showing traits of their unique personality type as young as preschool age.

In childhood, ENFPs lead predominantly with extroverted intuition. They make for excitable, energetic children who are insatiably curious about the world around them. This type grows into their introverted feeling in adolescence and their extroverted thinking and introverted sensing follow suit in early to late adulthood (The Myers & Briggs Foundation, 2015). For the first two to three decades of their lives, ENFPs are likely to be most aware of their extroverted intuition and introverted feeling, as they are the primary functions they rely on.

ENFPs In Childhood

In some ways, childhood fits the ENFP personality immensely. This type is energetic, extroverted, explorative and insatiably curious – all traits that are expected and revered in children.

In other ways, childhood has the potential to be a highly stressful experience for ENFPs. This type is both highly individualistic and highly independent. They dislike having limitations placed on their behaviors and may grow quickly frustrated with the lack of autonomy that childhood allows them. They may also experience conflict with family members who do not share the ENFP's preference for intuition or perception, as their needs will not necessarily align with those of the rest of their family's.

As children, ENFPs are:

- Highly energetic in early childhood.
- Eager to see, touch and experience everything for themselves.
- Quick to question or refute rules and limitations.
- Independent to a fault.
- Insatiably curious – constantly probing for the 'deeper meaning' behind everything they experience and perceive.
- Extremely sensitive to criticism of any sort.
- Openly sensitive and emotional.
- Usually growing shyer and more reserved as childhood progresses.

- Wildly fantasy prone.
- Extremely individualistic.
- Often distrustful of or defiant towards authority.
- Occasionally frustrated by their inability to express themselves properly.
- Resistant to adhering to routines or participating in monotonous activities (such as repetitive chores).

Common challenges ENFPs face in childhood:

- ENFPs are sharp and intelligent children, but they often feel unable to properly communicate their many ideas through the traditional education system.
- ENFP children may feel deeply misunderstood by their family or peers, who do not seem to think, feel or analyze anything as deeply as the ENFP does.
- ENFP children crave social interaction intensely but may feel shy and hesitant to initiate it.
- ENFP children may find themselves passionately interested in many subjects, but lacking the discipline or follow-through to pursue them to fruition.
- ENFPs learn through experience and may struggle with adhering to rules simply because they were told to do something a certain way.
- ENFPs have a short attention span and may experience difficulty paying attention in school or when working independently on assignments.
- ENFP children are highly perceptive of other

peoples' reactions to them. If those around them are unable to make sense of the ENFP's erratic behavior, the ENFP is quick to pick up on this and may internalize the feeling that they are different or that something is wrong with them.

- Many ENFP children feel as though they have a deeper, 'true' version of themselves hiding beneath the surface that nobody really understands or cares to get to know. This can be a lonely or isolating experience for the ENFP child.

Raising an ENFP Child

Bringing up an ENFP child is no easy feat. While these types are explorative, bright-eyed and sweet on their best days, they are bratty, temperamental and demanding on their worst. In raising an ENFP child, it is important to keep in mind that children of this type have two basic desires: To explore freely and to be understood deeply. The ENFP who feels supported, validated and understood by those around him or her is an ENFP who is likely to thrive.

Here are a few things to keep in mind if you are raising an ENFP child:

- Participate in long conversations with your ENFP child. To you, they may seem to be blabbering aimlessly but to them, they are sharing their thoughts with you in an attempt to make a genuine connection.

- ENFP children require an excessive amount of positive affirmation. Remind the ENFP on a daily basis that you love and care for them.
- Take a genuine interest in their hobbies and projects, no matter how short-lived they are.
- Understand that the ENFP child lacks follow-through, but that this will come with age. Pushing them to continue with activities they have lost interest in will likely be a fruitless endeavor.
- Help your ENFP child to work backwards from his or her big ideas. If they are working on a project, allow them to complete it out of order and then help them fill in the details as they go.
- Allow the ENFP to explore each of their wild, fanciful ideas. Wait until their initial excitement has subsided to discuss the concrete realities of their ideas with them.
- Work with your ENFP child to complete school assignments if he or she is having trouble focusing. This type responds particularly well to positive mentorship.
- Accept that the ENFP child is going to have to learn most lessons the hard way. Give them the space to (safely) make their mistakes.
- When they have done something wrong, take the time to explain to the ENFP why the thing they have done is wrong and how it hurts or negatively affects others.

- Allow a little disorganization in the ENFP's room. Clutter is psychologically comforting to this type in childhood and it's important for them to have a physical space they can retreat to and feel comfortable within.
- Engage the ENFP's spirit of adventure. Take them exploring to new areas of town or on small trips if you can afford it. This type thrives on exploration and a change in scenery is often all it takes to rejuvenate a distressed ENFP.

ENFPs As Teenagers

As ENFPs enter their teen years, their introverted feeling begins to develop in leaps and bounds. While late childhood may have presented a timid, shy version of the ENFP, their teenage years bring about a fiercely individualistic version. ENFP teenagers may feel overwhelmed by their sudden influx of emotion and feel genuinely out of control of their own mood swings.

As their introverted feeling develops, the ENFP's childish curiosity will morph into a philosophical exploration of the world around them. The ENFP teenager may find themselves probing each new experience for the 'deeper' meaning behind it. The more they take in, the more they will begin to form definitive thoughts and opinions on moral issues. They may become particularly defensive about their beliefs at this age and develop a keen argumentative streak.

In their late teen years, ENFPs will likely become preoccupied by visions of their adult life. They may feel frustrated and constrained by their lack of independence and wish desperately to get their 'real life' started. ENFP teens are likely to take an intense interest in the possibilities that exist for them in the future and may change their life plan an exorbitant amount of times, much to the distress of their parents and mentors.

Common challenges ENFPs face as teenagers:

- Experiencing intense emotional ups and downs that they feel largely unable to control.
- Wanting to be popular with peers but not wanting to compromise their core values or their authenticity.
- Experiencing difficulty balancing their need for social time with their newfound need for alone time.
- Feeling incredibly lonely or isolated if they lack intuitive friends or mentors.
- Growing into the understanding that they are 'not like' other people but failing to understand exactly why.
- Having a wide range of interests but lacking the follow-through to pursue any of them to fruition.
- Having a clear vision of what they'd like for the future but lacking the resources to pursue that vision.
- Possessing the ability to think deeply about complex

issues, but lacking the ability to convey their thoughts and opinions through a traditional system of education.

- Feeling wildly motivated yet intensely disorganized on a mental, physical and emotional level.
- The majority of issues that plague teenage ENFPs are born from their inability to concretely organize their emotions, visions and dreams. In their late teen years and throughout their twenties, ENFPs finally begin to develop extroverted thinking, which helps them to balance their erratic thoughts and emotions with concrete actions.

In the meantime, ENFP teens may benefit from seeking out an older mentor of their same personality type. This will help them to feel less isolated in their way of thinking and will also help them to understand how their wild ideals can be structured and carried out in an organized fashion.

ENFPs In Early Adulthood

"You must be the person you have never had the courage to be. Gradually, you will discover that you are that person, but until you can see this clearly, you must pretend and invent."
–Paulo Coelho

Early adulthood is usually a time of excitement and vast exploration for the ENFP. They are finally granted the independence they have longed for and they want to waste no time getting out and experiencing the world in full force.

Between the ages of 18 and 30, ENFPs develop their tertiary function, extroverted thinking. Extroverted thinking helps the ENFP balance their emotional highs and lows, organizes their visions into concrete actions and helps them to make confident decisions regarding their long-term goals and plans.

Of course, extroverted thinking does not develop all at once. The ENFP will likely spend their late teens and early twenties letting their extroverted intuition and introverted feeling run wild. They are likely to experiment with various partners, interests, beliefs, career paths, locations, ideals, identities and plans for the future. They may change their major several times in college. They may work countless different jobs in quick succession. They may fall in and out of love with various different people. The young adult ENFP is inspired by the world that surrounds him or her and wants to experience it all in full force.

Ironically, the rampant exploration of different thoughts and feelings is exactly what the ENFP needs in order to properly develop their tertiary extroverted thinking. The more experiences they take in, the greater their frame of experiential reference becomes and the more judgment they are able to apply to future decisions.

As the ENFP develops their extroverted thinking function, their behavior becomes steadily more focused and assertive. Rather than floundering from experience to experience, they will develop a clearer vision of what they want and will begin to develop a 'go-getter' attitude. The ENFP may find themselves able to make decisions and follow through on their goals for the first time in their lives. Though they will still be highly perceptive of the possibilities that are available to them, ENFPs will find it increasingly easier to make decisions and follow through on ideas as they age. This will likely come as a major relief to both the ENFP and those in their lives.

Though it is usually a time of exciting exploration for the ENFP, early adulthood is certainly not without its struggles.

Common challenges ENFPs face in early adulthood:

- Struggling to focus their attention throughout college or University in classes that are taught in a traditional lecture format.
- Struggling to commit to romantic relationships.
- Feeling indecisive about which educational or career path to follow.
- Tiring quickly of new jobs and relationships.
- Feeling limited by or resistant to the "9-5" workweek that they are expected to adhere to.

The majority of the challenges that ENFPs face in their twenties relate back to their inability to narrow down the excess of possibilities that are available to them. Though their extroverted thinking helps them to achieve the visions of what they want, they still have not fully developed their introverted sensing, which keeps them grounded and helps them to stick affirmatively to decisions.

ENFPs In Adulthood

From the age of approximately thirty onwards, ENFPs begin to develop their inferior function, introverted sensing. This function provides balance and direction to their dominant extroverted intuition and helps the ENFP to follow through on decisions and plans. In this phase of their lives, ENFPs may find themselves becoming increasingly able to stick with decisions and see their ideas through to fruition.

As they age, ENFPs will become increasingly comfortable with routine and traditional methods of accomplishing tasks. They may finally feel ready to settle down and start a family (if that is what they wish to do) or to pursue a single career path for an extended period of time.

The development of introverted sensing will also manifest in the form of health-consciousness – the ENFP will become increasingly perceptive of their physical needs and will likely begin taking significantly better care of their health. The ENFP is likely to feel steadily more at peace with themselves – both mentally and physically – as they age.

While adulthood brings about a variety of changes in the ENFP's erratic nature, this type does not ever grow out of their core personality. ENFPs will always be the passionate, eccentric, idealistic inspirers they were born as. And if they're being honest with themselves, they wouldn't have it any other way.

6

Growing Up Intuitive In A World Of Sensors

"Everybody is a genius. But if you judge a fish by its ability to climb a tree, it will live its whole life believing that it is stupid."
–Albert Einstein

Because sensing types make up the majority of the population, many young ENFPs find themselves being raised in families made up entirely of sensing types. While contrasts in personality can certainly be beneficial in many ways, young ENFPs often report feeling somewhat 'crazy' or out of place in their sensory-oriented families. They may feel similarly out of place at school or around peers – perceiving themselves to be slightly different from the majority of people around them, but not being able to pinpoint exactly how or why.

10 Things That Happen When You're An Intuitive In A Family Of Sensors

1. Whenever you asked "why" as a kid, you got a completely different answer than what you were expecting. When you asked, "why is the boy on TV sad," you already knew it was because someone kicked him. What you really wanted to know is why bad things happen to good people and whether or not there's a karmic balance to the Universe. Unfortunately it's difficult to phrase those questions when you are four.

2. So. Much. Family. Gossip. It's not that you don't want to know about what's going on with your family. It's just that you want to know different parts of what's going on with your family. "Your cousin Sally started working at the nursery!" Is not of great interest to you. What are Sally's aspirations? Where does she see herself in ten years? What is it about human nature that compels us to nurture our young with a sense of unending compassion? These seem to be more relevant questions. But we're already onto your cousin Kelly, who is dating someone new.

3. What you are doing will always be of infinitely greater interest to your family than what you are thinking. When your parents call, they want to know three things: Are you keeping warm, are you making enough money to remain alive and have you eaten any vegetables this week? What's on your mind is not important. It can be frustrating at times but you have to admit... you do occasionally forget to eat your veggies.

4. In order to be taken seriously, you have to show rather than tell. Sensors place more weight on what you do than what you talk about. So if you want your family to appreciate your interest in science, you're going to have to first achieve distinction from an accredited University and publish several wildly successful scientific papers. Then – and only then – will your family give weight to what you have to say about the scientific theory you've had the same opinion on for years.

5. Your definition of 'family bonding' is wildly different than your family's definition. Your definition of 'bonding time' involves sharing ideas, discussing theories and coming to deeply understand each other's core motivations and beliefs. Your family's definition of 'bonding time' is going ice-skating together. Tomato, tomato.

6. Trying to discuss your feelings is a stressful experience for everyone. For sensors, feelings are a matter of cause-and-effect. If you can't relate a particular feeling you're having to a specific, tangible experience that necessitated it, your family has a tough time understanding why you're feeling the way you are. The good news is, feelings are often related to specific, tangible events. And it may just take a conversation with a sensor to make you realize that your problem isn't quite as complex as you thought it was.

7. If you're not doing something physical, it's assumed you're doing nothing. Reading up on a topic that you're interested in is considered 'doing nothing' with your day. Going to soccer practice is considered doing something. Go figure.

8. You genuinely question your own sanity at times. Because they're highly in tune with their environments (at least compared to intuitives), sensors usually come off as significantly more levelheaded than intuitives. Intuitives spend their time wrapped up in the world of thoughts and possibilities – and can subsequently work themselves into mind funks that sensors just cannot... well, make sense of. When an intuitive spends enough time around non-intuitives, it becomes incredibly easy to start questioning their own sanity. After all, nobody else seems to be troubled by the sort of theoretical problems that keep you awake at night. Is something deeply wrong with you?

9. You relate so hard to Calvin in *Calvin & Hobbes* it hurts. Our favorite little ENTP comic-book character offers the perfect depiction of what it's like to be an N-dominant child growing up in a family of sensors. No wonder he had to imagine himself an intuitive tiger friend. We all could have used a little Hobbes growing up.

10. At the end of the day, you have to admit that you couldn't have done it without them. If there's anything we can all agree on, it's that the world needs a mix of both sensors and intuitives. And in your case, sensors are the reason you're the person you are today – they made sure you were fed, clothed, well-rested and cared for in a way that does not come naturally to you. And it's hard to complain about that.

30 ENFPs Share What They'd Tell Their Younger Selves

"Don't waste your time trying to live an average life. You aren't average. And that is your greatest advantage."

"Some people are going to like your chipper personality and enthusiasm, some people are going to be really annoyed by it. Don't let the people who don't like you change who you are. In order to meet people like yourself, you have to act like yourself."

"The insights your intuition gives you are valid even if others can't comprehend them and you're not really aware of how you know them either."

"YOU ARE NOT CRAZY. I promise."

"There are many, many awesome people out there who will get you. They might space out their arrivals but they're coming."

"Never be ashamed of being passionate about everything. Or getting excited about all of the things. Fall leaves? EXCITED. Animals? EXCITED. My enthusiasm is invigorating. Those who can't handle it will eventually stay away and that's 100% okay."

"For some people it IS better to do a hundred things with mediocrity than one thing to an exceptional level."

"The things you naturally excel at cannot be taught in school or tested on an exam."

"That the reason you can't plan an essay the way that others do isn't because your mind goes blank – but because thinks of too much at once and explodes in all directions. Get a sheet of paper (or a blank screen) and write down ALL of it, even the stupid stuff that seems irrelevant. It's far easier to rearrange from something than nothing. Start in the middle, work backwards, forwards and sideways. Because if you try to start at the beginning, you'll never write anything."

"You don't have ADHD, you have ENFP."

"It's okay, nay, essential to live by who you are instead of conforming to other's perceptions of what you should be. Being scattered doesn't mean you're messed up, being excited about everything doesn't make you shallow, and wanting to go everywhere doesn't make you short-sighted. There are strengths in all of these places that you will eventually embrace as some of your greatest talents!"

"It's OK to be a big feeler. You don't need to learn to 'feel less', but rather how to effectively manage feeling everything in life on a big scale."

"You don't have to be best friends with EVERYBODY. Alone time is both important and necessary to your mental health."

"Trust your gut about what you want to do in life. You will regret listening to those who push you toward a more 'dependable' degree."

"Although you are easily distracted and have a short attention span, you have the ability to be incredibly productive when you decide to. You can accomplish all of your goals, as long as you REALLY put yourself up to the task."

"Something good for the world can come from you, not just in spite of your differences, but because of them."

"Just because your family doesn't understand you and thinks something is seriously wrong with you, doesn't mean it's true. It's hard, not being able to trust your own parents like that, but don't let it get you down or keep you shy and silent. Know that you can take your life into your own hands."

"You are not wrong or bad. Your nature isn't bad. You are not a bad person."

"You will be restless your entire life… and that doesn't make you crazy. You fit in everywhere but don't fit in anywhere… and that doesn't make you crazy. You see the world completely differently than most people, which means most people won't get you… but that doesn't make you crazy. Just because you don't function well in the traditional education system, doesn't make you unintelligent…nor does it make you crazy."

"It is entirely plausible to be a shy extrovert. That doesn't mean that there's anything wrong with you!"

"One day you will find other intuitive people who will love you and accept you for who you are and they will encourage you to be the best and truest you, you can be."

"It's totally fine to feel joyful one moment, then morose the next. It's completely fine to crave for some adrenaline or any sense of adventure one day, and seek for solitude and silence the next. No matter how contradicting you feel you are towards your own feelings and emotions, deep down, you truly possess a strong and vibrant personality, while being sensitive and artistic at the same time. Ultimately, you are unique, highly imaginative, inspiring, overwhelming and simply awesome as an ENFP."

"Your definition of success is different than other peoples. For some, it's about the money in their pay check. For you, it's about happiness, well-being, morality and passion."

"It's okay to not want stability and to long for excitement. It's also okay to crave stability deep down. It is possible to find a balance, it just may take a long time to achieve it."

"The grass is always going to look greener, even when your own lawn is luscious."

"It's ok to be so much more introverted than other extroverts and to need to crawl into your little cave after intense communication. Fluctuations in mood and energy are natural to your type. You shouldn't force yourself to enjoy Excel tables and schedules and planned tasks, but focus on your personal strengths instead. Order and predictability are not your cup of tea. You can achieve more by inspiring and supporting your peers and subordinates than by trying to bite off more than you can personally chew."

"It's okay to get excited and passionate about ALL the things and keep moving through new ideas. The best ideas will stick around."

"Just because your thought process is different doesn't mean it's any less valid. You're smarter than yourself and others think."

"THERE ISN'T ANYTHING WRONG WITH YOU. Your wanderlust isn't something that you need to beat down. Your constant need for stimulation doesn't make you stupid. You're just a person who needs to be constantly engaged with life."

"It is possible to find peace within the chaos of your mind."

Part 3

ENFPs In The Workplace

7

ENFPs At Work

"Don't ask yourself what the world needs. Ask yourself what makes you come alive, and go do it. Because what the world needs is people who have come alive."
–Howard Thurman

ENFPs approach work the way they approach everything else – with optimism, enthusiasm and determination.

True to the ENFP form, this type is all about variety in the workplace. Many ENFPs find it difficult to choose just one career path and they may elect to change fields various times over the span of their professional lives. Because they are motivated by challenge and authenticity, the ENFP is likely to excel in just about any role that they feel strongly about.

ENFPs commonly report being employed in the following fields:

- Counseling
- Education
- Marketing
- Entrepreneurship
- Human Resources

- Journalism
- Ministry
- Academia

While one's Myers-Briggs type can certainly reveal a great deal about one's strengths and weaknesses in the workplace, it doesn't particularly help discriminate which career path would be best suited for each type. The ENFP in particular may experience a great deal of confusion over which field to choose, as many of them tend to be a "Jack of all trades, master of none."

Luckily, this type possesses a strong drive to excel. Because they are incredibly self-motivated, the single most important aspect for any ENFP to consider while choosing a career path is whether or not their chosen profession excites and inspires them. If so, the ENFP will do whatever it takes to excel in the workplace. If not, they are unlikely to last long in the field.

Regardless of which career path they choose, there are a few crucial components that the ENFP requires from their workplace in order to stay engaged and involved day to day.

What Every ENFP Needs From Their Career

1. Challenge And Variety.

It's no secret that ENFPs bore quickly. In order to thrive

professionally, this type is best suited for a role that provides them with a steady stream of novel challenges to rise to. They feel invigorated by taking on new clients, projects and cases. This type never wants to have the same workday twice!

2. External Structure.

Though their own work tends to be creative and unstructured, ENFPs actually function best within a system of external order. As long as they are given autonomy, most ENFPs report thriving in workplaces that are predominantly made up of judgers. The structure that judgers create is comforting to the ENFP and it allows them to fully engage their creative side.

Additionally, follow-through is not the ENFP's strong suit. The ideal workplace for this type is one in which they can serve as an idea-generator and their more routine-oriented coworkers can see those ideas to fruition.

3. Autonomy.

ENFPs despise feeling constrained or controlled in any way, so having autonomy in the workplace is an absolute must for them. Many ENFPs choose to enter into entrepreneurial fields and work as their own bosses. Others seek out positions that allow them the opportunity to thrive creatively under loose supervision. Because this type is so self-motivated, they often require very little supervision in the workplace. They are best suited with an employer who understands and appreciates this!

4. Connection.

The ideal career for an ENFP is one that makes them feel as though they're making a genuine difference in the lives of others. ENFPs thrive on connection – they seek to form meaningful relationships with their clients and coworkers alike, in order to help them in as significant a manner as possible. Isolated, technical or impersonal work is likely to drain the ENFP over an extended period of time.

5. Authenticity.

Above all else, the ENFP needs to feel as though they're staying true to themselves through their work. This type is governed by a strong set of morals, which urges them to make a difference in the world in whichever way they personally see fit. ENFPs are big-picture people, who need to feel connected to and motivated by their job on a personal level. If they perceive their work to be meaningful, they'll throw their all into it. Otherwise, they'll waste no time leaving to pursue a new career.

Strengths Of The ENFP In The Workplace

ENFPs make for dedicated, passionate and all-around delightful workers. They are highly inventive individuals who are intrinsically motivated to realize their full potential professionally.

Bosses and co-workers alike tend to rave about their ENFP colleagues, who go out of their way to make the workplace an enjoyable place to be for everyone. Some of the key strengths that ENFPs bring to the workplace are as follows:

- ENFPs are incredibly adaptable and can pick up a wide range of new skills with ease.
- ENFPs are friendly and charming; possessing the unique ability to make coworkers and clients feel comfortable around them almost instantly.
- ENFPs love a challenge and will work tirelessly toward absolutely any goal that inspires them.
- ENFPs are creative thinkers who are skilled at contriving novel solutions to complex problems.
- ENFPs tend to personally invest themselves in their workplace and they make for loyal and driven employees.
- ENFPs are highly independent workers who require little instruction or motivation to get a job done well.
- ENFPs possess the impressive ability to analyze all sides of a given situation and see the 'bigger picture', which helps them get down to the heart of important matters quickly.
- ENFPs are highly enthusiastic and are particularly adept at riling up and motivating other workers.
- ENFPs make for confident and enthusiastic presenters, who feel at ease in front of a crowd.
- ENFPs think best on their feet and work well under pressure. When a job needs to get done quickly, creatively and effectively, you want an ENFP on your team!

Challenges The ENFP Faces In The Workplace

Like any other type, ENFPs face a unique set of challenges in the workplace. While they do make for dedicated and enthusiastic workers, this type tends to struggle with diligence and follow-through in the workplace. A few of the challenges ENFPs may face in their professional lives are as follows:

- ENFPs strongly dislike repetitive tasks and may struggle to continuously perform the mundane aspects of their jobs.
- ENFPs thrive when they are given autonomy and may feel stifled while working under close supervision.
- ENFPs may experience difficulty prioritizing tasks, as they tend to gravitate toward the ones that they find the most interesting, regardless of their urgency.
- ENFPs may get sidetracked while working on long-term projects and experience difficulty following them through to fruition.
- ENFPs may over-estimate their abilities and bite off more than they can chew in the workplace.
- ENFPs are highly sensitive to criticism and may struggle with receiving negative feedback in the workplace.
- ENFPs may experience difficulty adhering to deadlines and fail to complete projects within the expected timeframe.
- In positions of management, the ENFP may struggle to provide an adequate amount of structure to

subordinates who require a high level of instruction and supervision.

- If they fail to find their career adequately challenging or interesting, the ENFP is likely to leave their job to pursue alternate possibilities. They will do this as many times as necessary and are at risk of spending the majority of their professional lives hopping from job to job.

Tips For Workplace Success as an ENFP

- **Work backwards from your big ideas.** ENFPs tend to grasp the big picture with ease, but have trouble narrowing their visions down into smaller, workable doses. Rather than attempting to complete projects in a linear manner (that is, starting at the beginning and following it sequentially to completion), the ENFP may benefit from starting with their biggest, 'meatiest' ideas and allowing the details to fall naturally into place as they go.

- **Surround yourself with coworkers whose strengths are your weaknesses.** Some of the greatest assets any ENFP has in the workplace are their colleagues. The ENFP is a natural team player and they are likely to benefit immensely from combining their big-picture ideals with the detail-orientation and follow-through of sensing, judging types. By surrounding themselves with those whose strengths are their weakness (and vice versa), the ENFP will set themselves up for professional success.

- **Break long-term tasks down into a series of mini-challenges.** ENFPs who are faced with long-term tasks may quickly lose interest and fall victim to intense bouts of procrastination. To avoid this, the ENFP can break long-term tasks down into a series of small challenges – each of which has a strict due date. They will keep themselves inspired by the challenge of rising to each new task and completing it under the pressure of an upcoming deadline.

- **Hold yourself publicly accountable for following through on projects.** Since disciplining themselves to follow through on long-term goals may be difficult for the ENFP, they may elect to hold themselves publicly accountable for completing mini-tasks. Because the ENFP hates letting others down, he or she is likely to feel particularly motivated to complete a task if others are holding them accountable for it.

- **Learn to embrace and grow from criticism.** When receiving constructive criticism from colleagues or bosses, keep in mind that they are providing you with feedback because they value your work and see opportunities for growth within you. They are harnessing your positive potential! Try to momentarily detach from criticism when you receive it – look at the objective facts that are being presented to you and visualize the opportunities for advancement that exist within them. If you are able to turn feedback into a challenge to rise to, it may help you feel inspired rather than offended by it.

- **Play from your strengths.** While setting deadlines, receiving criticism and surrounding oneself with judging types are likely to aid the ENFP throughout the course of their career, the most important thing to keep in mind is that in order to flourish professionally, the ENFP needs to choose a role that maximizes their strengths. This type feeds off positive energy, so the more they are able to accomplish from a place of authenticity, the better they will be at dealing with the mundane aspects of their job. When they throw their heart fully into work, the ENFP is capable of excelling at just about any career they choose.

8

ENFP Testimonials

"A human being should be able to change a diaper,
plan an invasion, butcher a hog, conn a ship,
design a building, write a sonnet, balance
accounts, build a wall, set a bone, comfort the
dying, take orders, give orders, cooperate, act
alone, solve equations, analyze a new problem,
pitch manure, program a computer, cook a tasty
meal, fight efficiently and die gallantly.
Specialization is for insects."
–Robert A. Heinlein

Rather than compiling a list of possible career choices for the ENFP (because the list would be endless), I decided to go straight to the horse's mouth and ask other ENFPs what they're currently doing for work. Unsurprisingly, the jobs were incredibly varied – ENFPs seem to be represented in almost every field imaginable.

What most of the responses did have in common was this – almost every ENFP was happy with the career they'd chosen. Many reported a history of changing jobs before finding the one that worked best for them. ENFPs are willing to attempt, experiment and move from job to job until they eventually find what works. And once they do, they hit their stride with ease. ENFPs make for passionate workers who consider their jobs to be an extension of themselves.

"I'm currently working as a social worker in addictions counseling. I'm very happy to see such intimate sides of people and support them in their growth. I draw a sense of meaning out of being that close to life – all of its beauty and its ugliness. After all, my greatest aspiration is to make my community a better place to be in."
–Salome, 26

"I'm a property developer! I love spotting opportunities, designing floor plans and doing interior design – these components engage my extroverted intuition and introverted feeling. The camaraderie on site is fun and things can progress very quickly! I have a great team of guys who do the skilled labor and co-ordination. Every day is different and I love running spontaneous errands, designing, creative problem solving and being adaptable. I also manage the budget, which is challenging but rewarding. It engages my extroverted thinking and introverted sensing."
–Sarah, 40

"I'm a grad student in music, but I also work as a career advisor for undergrad students in the College of Arts and Humanities at my university. I work with students to find them internships and I critique resumes and cover letters. I love the job because it is constantly changing and there's always something new to do! I'm still just finishing my training, but already I've sat in on student appointments with my boss and started editing stuff myself. I've also gotten to write promo tweets for our upcoming events, and done some Internet sleuthing to compile contact info for arts directors from local colleges. There's enough variety to keep me from getting bored and I thrive on all the people interaction. It also helps that everyone in my office is SUPER friendly and fun to work with! I'm fairly certain that my job is ENFP heaven."

-Devon, 25

"I started my career as a radio DJ and loved it. Being live on air allowed me to be very spontaneous – I had no set playlist and could play whatever I felt like on any particular day. I then continued on with music journalism. But eventually bills needed paying and music journalism alone wasn't an option as a career, so I did "classical" newsroom journalism for several years, eventually ascending to the managing editor position. I didn't fully enjoy newsroom work. Producing a daily paper is boring – it's a routine like factory work or accounting. Finally I switched to PR – doing agency work, which is almost never boring – and have been doing it for 8 years now. This work always encouraged me to hop from one subject to the next in no time at all – like giving a lecture on media and public performance for Estonian Bar Association in the morning, consulting a construction company in the afternoon and mixing smoothies at the home appliances' client event in the evening. I love my job, I really do, it pays really well, I love my colleagues and clients, my boss is the best ever, etc. But

more often than not I keep asking myself: 'Is that all there is?'"
–Alex, 34

"I'm a former preschool owner and teacher. I loved it because I truly love my little ones and their families! I'm fiercely independent and I loved owning my own business and the ability to teach the way I feel is best! I also loved being able to hand pick the people I worked with. I truly love every single one of my employees! I could NEVER work in a public school or even in someone else's classroom. I'm not a big rule-follower. I just don't do bosses…"
–Amanda, 37

"I'm an executive level public servant with the Australian army. I manage safety risk and corporate governance. I'm not the usual 'audit' type – I mentor, encourage and have a 'teach them to fish' attitude. Eventually my subordinates will be able to do what they need without me. If I do it for them they'll never learn!"
–Janna, 52

"I work in the special education department at an elementary school. I love my job because everyday is something new! There are no monotonous tasks, I get to be around people, and every minute my passion grows for kids with special needs. My job is perfect for ENFPs because situations aren't black and white for us – and when it comes to special ed, NOTHING is absolute. Every child, situation, education plan, ability level, behavior, preferred item, and

personality is different and in a constant state of change with these kids. In my job, it's an asset to think from every angle, not a hindrance! Plus I get to see beautiful smiles and get to help grow beautiful minds. It's so rewarding. My heart is full at the end of each day!"
–Sarah, 22

"I'm a pastry chef. This job is great for ENFP because it is a lot of multitasking and the job is different every day. I also get to be creative and am constantly learning new techniques!"
–Carrie, 39

"I'm the associate editor for an online travel publication! I love my job because no day is ever the same. It allows me to write about my passion and create my own routine – in other words, I have a flexible schedule and never feel trapped in the day to day. I also get to meet a ton of interesting people who I consider BEST FRIENDS FOREVER throughout the industry. The only downside is that my wanderlust is constantly at an all-time high; I wish I could just up and leave whenever I want, and book a spontaneous flight somewhere. But what ENFP doesn't?!"
-Gina, 28

"I work in the emergency room as a tech and enjoy every minute of it because I get to meet a ton of new patients on a daily basis. Also, it is great because there is a near infinite amount of real work that has to be done, but isn't set in a required fashion (i.e. do CPR at 8am). It's great because I have the freedom to choose how to best make an impact in my patients' lives. With this job it is impossible to predict what type of day I will have and love every minute of it. Another part that I love about my job is the team aspect. There are so many people like me who hate draconian-like rules. We all get each other, and "Play nice" together. Work really doesn't feel like work. It feels like fun!"

–Trevor, 24

"I work as the executive director for a non-profit that focuses on addressing root-causes for major issues impacting our community. I love what I do because it doesn't feel like a job; I get paid to be me! Every day is unique and I love that there's so much creativity involved in problem solving. Parts of my job require me to tap into the areas of my personality that I don't use as my go-to in my personal life."

–Katie, 35

"I'm a Customer Success Manager for a software startup. I do customer training and implementation, consulting and analysis, and account management. It's a small enough company that I get to wear a ton of hats instead of being pigeonholed. My work involves all the things on which I thrive: problem-solving, complexity, variety, people-pleasing, analysis, writing, editing, tenacity, adaptability, strategy, and public speaking. My job works well with my weaknesses, too – my inability to work in a linear fashion, my struggle to focus. I tend to be the "catalyst" of the team, the passionate one drawing attention to unrecognized problems and driving

new approaches."
–Kira, 28

"I am a somewhat shy ENFP who is a pastor, and have been for 37 years. I love my work for the most part. It has lots of variety. I love that while my weeks have a rhythm to them, each day has variety. I get to be creative and think about the big picture. While the details can drive me bananas, I make sure the ones that are really important get done, and emphasize that to others on my staff. I have worked hard to have integrity in my life, including how I am in public. I regard my leadership, in preaching and other activities, as primarily about directing people's focus through me to God."
–Mochel, 61

"I just completed my master of marketing and am a marketing manager for a small firm. I do all the marketing, as well as their regulatory, as well as their pricing, as well as whatever they need me to do. It's a nicely diverse roll. I try to be stable, but change jobs on a regular basis. BK (before kids) it was about every three years, now it is about every five. Until now, I have always moved around within the company, going for a new role every year or two. I have been at my current company for about three years, and I am getting seriously itchy feet!"
–Kendel, 48

"Some days I'm a writer. Others, a musician. Some days, I paint. I also have a bartending license. Okay, so maybe I haven't exactly figured out my "calling" but I'm okay with that. I like that I am able to be the jack of all trades and enjoy being multi-talented, and spend my "youth" doing things that I really enjoy. Stuff will fall into place when it's meant to."

–Lianna, 24

9

Defining Your Core Values

ENFPs are known for their strict adherence to a set of core values, and they often base their choice of career off the values that are most important to them. But what if you aren't sure what your own core values are?

The following questions exist to serve as prompts for helping you uncover your core values. Think carefully about which values you are expressing in each of your answers and keep an eye out for any trends that emerge as you go.

1. Write down 1-5 traits that make you incredibly angry when you see them in other people. Then, write down which value each of these people are violating through the behavior you've listed.

e.g. "Narrow-mindedness in others offends me because it violates the values of kindness and open-mindedness."

2. Write down the three things you're proudest of yourself for having accomplished in life thus far. Then, write down which values were exemplified through those victories.

e.g. "I am proud of having traveled the world on my own,

because independence and exploration are values that are important to me."

e.g. "I'm proud of having raised my daughter into a kind, compassionate young woman because supporting and nurturing others is one of my core values."

3. Write down what your greatest failure has been so far in life. Reflect on what it was about that experience that made it feel like a failure, and what the corresponding core value is.

e.g. "My marriage felt like a failure because I couldn't give my ex-husband the support he needed from me. Supporting others is one of my core values."

e.g. "Not getting into graduate school was a failure for me because I felt as though I wouldn't be allotted the opportunity to continue to learn. Intellectual growth is a value of mine."

4. Write down three of the happiest experiences of your life so far. Then, identify what all of these experiences have in common, and what the corresponding core value is.

e.g. "My wedding day, my first year of University and traveling across Asia were some of the happiest experiences of my life. In all of those instances, I was taking on new challenges and was surrounded by loved ones. Challenging myself is a core value of mine, as is maintaining a community."

5. Write down the names of three people you admire and list the traits you admire them for. Then, identify which – if any – traits all of those people share.

e.g. "I admire my mom – for being nurturing to me at my

worst, my Professor – for believing in each of his students even when they're doing poorly and my boss – for driving the company to success after a failed first year. All of those people show persistence in the face of adversity. Resilience is a core value of mine. "

Now, review the core values you listed in your answers to each question. Which ones show up several times? Which ones pop out at you as most important or significant? The answers that feel most authentic and genuine to you are indicative of your core values. They are what you ought to keep in mind and reference while you are making decisions and planning for the future – they indicate what is most important to you in life.

10

ENFPs And Follow-Through

Motivation is a tricky subject for any type – but ENFPs in particular have a difficult time staying committed to the follow-through of their many ideas. In the workplace, this may hinder the ENFP's ability to complete long-term projects. On a personal level, it may affect their ability to achieve long-term goals.

The ENFP's trouble with follow-through stems predominantly from the combination of extroverted intuition and introverted feeling. Extroverted intuition conceives of an invigorating new idea and conveys it to introverted feeing. Introverted feeling then acts as a decision-making function and gives extroverted intuition the go-ahead to get started on its new project – at which point extroverted intuition does all the 'fun parts' of the project, then loses interest and begins perusing alternate ideas to get excited about.

Though generally fruitless, this process is highly energizing for the ENFP in the short term, as the excitement of a new idea provides a temporary high that is difficult to match. If, however, the cycle goes on for too long, the ENFP is at risk of starting and stopping a seemingly infinite number of new endeavors.

In the long-term, this weighs heavily on the ENFP's introverted feeling as they find themselves lacking the deep sense of underlying meaning that they so desperately crave. ENFPs must find a way to remain focused on long-term projects in a way that does not drain and deplete their natural source of exuberance. Luckily, there are ways to strike that happy medium.

Step 1: Activate your extroverted thinking during your initial surge of inspiration.

For ENFPs, almost every new project begins as a grandiose burst of inspiration. We come up with a fantastic new idea and immediately jump into researching, planning and working toward whatever new idea has struck our fancy. Of course, this level of energy is wholly unsustainable. It won't get us all the way to our goal, but we can use it as an excellent kick-start by engaging our extroverted thinking alongside our extroverted intuition when inspiration hits.

Our extroverted thinking enjoys working with our extroverted intuition to figure out how we can make our grandiose ideas happen, which is what we must take advantage of during this phase. During our initial surge of inspiration, it is important that we source tangible methods of working toward our goal. We can use the 'inspired phase' to map out a series of mini-challenges that can be followed up on as we move methodically toward the over-arching goal.

Step 2: Learn to narrow down big picture.

We are big picture people – this is both our greatest strength and our greatest weakness when it comes to accomplishing goals. We fixate on the big picture when we take on new projects and consequently give up on them once the main points are covered and only the details remain.

Counter-intuitive as it seems, we often have to put the big picture on the back burner to achieve a realistic shot at achieving our long-term goals. Our introverted feeling provides a small-scale need for validation and if we rest the fulfillment of that need upon the achievement of a long-term goal, we will become quickly disheartened in the process of working toward it. To counter this effect, we must set up our goal as a series of mini-challenges that can be risen to regularly.

Step 3: Break your goals down into manageable portions.

ENFPs tend to take a top-down approach to accomplishing things: We identify an exciting opportunity via our extroverted intuition, decide to go for it via our introverted feeling and then source the necessary resources via our extroverted thinking. We then trust that our introverted sensing will continue to perform the actions necessary to get us all the way to our goal. And this is where we are being unrealistic.

We forget that we dislike relying on our introverted sensing unless we can identify the concrete payoff of doing so. In many ways, we must use our introverted sensing as a "swivel point" in accomplishing our goals – we cannot rely on it to take us all the way to the end, but we can use it to feed back into our extroverted thinking, introverted feeling and extroverted intuition as we work toward an ever-changing version of our overarching goal. In many ways, we need to work down and then back up in our stack of functions in order to keep ourselves motivated. The process may look a little like this:

Ne: Identifies an exciting opportunity.
Fi: Decides the opportunity is worth pursuing.
Te: Sources necessary resources for accomplishing goal.
Si: Repetitively performs the action that will bring us toward goal.
Te: Recognizes the immediate payoff of action that is being performed.
Fi: Feels validated based on our mini accomplishment.
Ne: Re-adjusts to identify the next challenge.

Repeat as necessary.

Examples:

Example 1: Setting a goal to lose weight.
Ne: Identifies the desire to lose weight and envisions various ways to go about doing so (i.e. Taking kick-boxing lessons, restricting caloric intake, etc.)
Fi: Imagines self at goal weight and decides that losing weight is worth doing.

Te: Roots through the ideas that Ne has presented and decides which specific methods will be employed (i.e. Decides to go kickboxing three times per week and restrict calorie intake to 1500 calories/day). Sets up a timeline for these goals, and sets a check in date.

Si: For the next month, goes kickboxing three times per week and restricts calorie intake to 1500 calories/day.

Te: Checks in after one month on progress. Notes changes (i.e. Ten pounds have been lost).

Fi: Feels validated based on progress.

Ne: Recognizes boredom with kickboxing and speculates new ways of losing weight (i.e. Taking up running, trying a juice cleanse, etc.).

Repeat process until desired amount of weight has been lost.

Example 2: Setting a goal to write a book.

Ne: Identifies the over-arching goal of writing a book and brainstorms different topics (i.e. A self-help book, a horror novel, a memoir).

Fi: Envisions oneself having achieved the goal of writing a book and identifies the positive emotions it would elicit – decides it is worth it to write the book.

Te: Narrows down the book topic and maps out specific chapters or drafts a skeleton.

Si: Writes several chapters.

Te: Checks in on progress and confirms whether or not book is progressing according to schedule.

Fi: Evaluates what has been written for authenticity and identifies areas that are not in line with the overall message that the book is trying to convey.

Ne: Brainstorms new ideas for content that would tie the book together and convey the intended message.

Repeat process until book has been completed.

Know When You're Fighting The Wrong Battle

As with anything, we have to pick our battles when it comes to our attention span. The development of our inferior functions (which is theorized to be complete around middle age) certainly helps, but it will not alter your personality completely. We are always going to be extroverted-intuition dominants. We are always going to be people-people. It's important to recognize when you require a bit of extra focus in order to complete a task you feel strongly about and when you're simply trying to complete a task that doesn't inspire or entice you. You are always going to work best when you're inspired by the task at hand – and if you're not, your efforts may be put to infinitely better use elsewhere.

Part 4

Unhealthy ENFP Behaviors

11

The Dark Side of the ENFP

Life as an ENFP is not all sunshine and roses. Despite the carefree attitude that ENFPs naturally exude, our feelings run deep and our health has the potential to plummet, as with any other type. In the following chapter, we'll explore the 'dark side' of the ENFP personality type – what happens when our psychological defenses break down and a reliance on our inferior function manifests.

How Your Greatest Strengths Are Also Your Greatest Weaknesses

To an extent, all personality traits exist on a spectrum. Unchecked assertiveness veers into aggression. Unbridled passion bleeds into obsession. And with a personality as strong as the ENFP's, there are a seemingly infinite number of traits that can manifest in vastly different ways as this type moves through various levels of health.

Below, we'll examine the various manifestations of some of the most common ENFP traits as they pertain to an optimally healthy and an unhealthy version of the type. In the following descriptions, the word "Healthy" is interchangeable (but not synonymous) with the word "Mature" and the word "Unhealthy" is interchangeable (but not synonymous) with the word "Immature."

Healthy	Unhealthy
Explorative	**Indecisive**
A healthy ENFP explores various ideas, plans and possibilities before narrowing down which ones to pursue to fruition.	An unhealthy ENFP pursues a seemingly endless flow of new ideas and lacks the ability to decide on or follow through with any of them.
Engaged	**Flakey**
A healthy ENFP has a lot on the go – they are always pursuing a new project, but they remain engaged with and committed to their undertakings.	An unhealthy ENFP is quick to abandon projects, plans and relationships as soon as they perceive a better option – often offering little or no explanation to others.
Understanding	**Manipulative**
A healthy ENFP uses their ability to see things from various points of view as a method of empathizing deeply with others.	An unhealthy ENFP uses their ability to see things from various points of view as a method of manipulating others to their own advantage.
Reflective	**Reclusive**
A healthy ENFP needs alone time to recharge and reflect on their emotions.	An unhealthy ENFP avoids social interaction in favor of stewing or obsessing over their feelings.

Principled

A healthy ENFP relies on their personal morals to govern their behavior and make important decisions.

Agreeable

A healthy ENFP makes reasonable compromises to make their loved ones happy.

Creative

A healthy ENFP is highly creative and artistic. They enjoy sharing their work with others and are enthusiastic about the work of fellow artists.

Loving

A healthy ENFP is openly affectionate towards their loved ones but respects their personal boundaries.

Self-Righteous

An unhealthy ENFP shames or looks down upon others for not abiding by their personal set of morals.

A Pushover

An unhealthy ENFP sacrifices his or her own needs in order to please others.

Pretentious

An unhealthy ENFP thrives on the idea of being misunderstood. They are hesitant to share their work with others and judge fellow artists harshly.

Clingy

An unhealthy ENFP is reliant on external validation and may ignore the boundaries of their loved ones to glean additional attention from them.

Autonomous
A healthy ENFP is highly independent and resourceful.

Enthusiastic
A healthy ENFP approaches new projects energetically and optimistically. They are 'big picture' thinkers who can quickly pick out which parts of a project are most important.

Supportive
A healthy ENFP aims to inspire his or her loved ones and genuinely wants to see them reach their full potential.

Controlling
An unhealthy ENFP is rigid, controlling and consumed by the need to maintain personal control of their external environment.

Obsessive
An unhealthy ENFP becomes obsessed with new ideas and projects. They may abandon their physical needs and work themselves into the ground trying to get everything done.

Jealous
An unhealthy ENFP wants to be the most impressive person in a given group and feels petty or jealous toward anyone who surpasses them.

As you can see, many common ENFP traits are a double-edged sword. A healthy, mature ENFP looks significantly different than an unhealthy, immature version of the same type. In the following chapters, we'll explore how the ENFP personality type manifests under situations of extreme pressure and periods of prolonged stress.

12

Times Of Trouble: How The Shadow Functions Manifest

First of all, let's clear up a few definitions.

In the type world, the term 'Shadow Functions,' is regularly used to describe two different manifestations of personality.

In some cases, the term 'Shadow Functions' is used to describe the functions that do not appear in a given personality type's stacking. As mentioned before, each type is capable of accessing all eight functions, but those that do not appear in one's main stacking will quickly drain the individual of energy. By this definition, the ENFP's shadow functions would be introverted intuition, extroverted feeling, introverted thinking and extroverted sensing – in order of how accessible they are to the ENFP.

The term 'Shadow Functions' as we will use it in the following chapter is used to describe the reversal of one's initial four-function stacking that occurs when a given type experiences stress. In the ENFP's case, this means we would cease to use Ne, Fi, Te and Si – in that order – and instead filter experiences through the lens of Si, then Te, then Fi and then Ne. This resembles the ISTJ's natural stack of cognitive functions. However, as introverted sensing tends to be underdeveloped in ENxP types, it does not manifest positively as a lead function, the way it does for an ISTJ.

The following chapter will explore the ENFP's descent into their shadow functions, as well as provide an explanation for how introverted sensing manifests as the ENFP's lead function during times of extreme stress. It will also detail the steps involved in the ENFP's return to health, as they integrate introverted sensing into their cognitive stacking in a healthy and well-rounded manner.

Introverted sensing is a wonderful, nourishing function that can help you achieve your full potential as an ENFP. When managed effectively, it will maintain your health, provide you with stability and help you to thrive in a world full of sensors.

When neglected, however, introverted sensing will take over in times of extreme stress and single-handedly ruin your life.

Introverted sensing means well. It really does. It is the lifejacket we keep in our back pocket just in case the ship starts going down. The problem is, as ENFPs, we are so concerned with what is in our front pockets that we tend to forget to take the life jacket out every now and again to check for holes. So when the ship starts going down (and at some point it will), we are left with an inconsistent lifesaving device.

Just like a faulty lifejacket forces you to use your valuable energy thrashing around in the water just trying to stay afloat, unhealthy introverted sensing does the bare minimum to keep our heads above water. The better we are at managing our Si in good health, the better we will be at catapulting ourselves out of ruts when they come up – because we won't have to spend all of our energy simply trying to stay afloat using underdeveloped Si.

When the ENFP ship starts sinking, our cognitive functions all jump in to try and save the day. Many times, this works. Our extroverted intuition is the superhero that pulls us from the majority of the troublesome scenarios we find ourselves in, before they get the chance to spiral out of control. Introverted feeling functions as the helpful sidekick and even the vigilante extroverted thinking works as our anti-hero when we need it most. Many times, introverted sensing doesn't even get the chance to step up to bat.

There is a specific series of events that leads us to the point where introverted sensing takes over – it isn't always straightforward or linear, but we do always pass through our first three functions to get there. Here is the descent that spirals the ENFP into ill health and calls their inferior function into action.

Stage 1: Extroverted Intuition Fails

Extroverted intuition is our executive function. It's the CEO of our minds and it tends to be a micromanager. At the first sign of trouble, Ne's there – as it should be. It's the function that keeps us afloat. Our first reaction to everything is to envision and theorize our way out of trouble.

The thing about Ne is that it kind of likes it when things go wrong – it sees everything in life as a challenge. This is what makes us one of the most optimistic types as well as one of the most self-destructive. Ne likes to knock things down for the simple sake of building them back up. Ne is eager to get its hands dirty.

So when we're encountering trouble, Ne riles. After getting fired or dumped or duped, the ENFP may actually feel more inspired than they do drained. Their first instinct will be to envision the various possibilities that lie ahead – new dreams, new goals, new opportunities that were previously not available to them. Failure is but another challenge to rise to and ENFPs like a challenge. Our initial reaction to something going wrong may be a powerful rush of adrenaline – it is Ne's time to shine and we let it, full force.

The problem is, Ne cannot pull us out of everything. The smaller the problem, the more likely that Ne can superhero it – it may jump in to help us find a new job and then pass the reigns over to introverted feeling to ask us how we're liking the environment and consult extroverted thinking to make sure we're keeping on top of the workload. Ne is a short-lived but powerful function that works best when it is balanced out by our lesser three functions.

When we become over-reliant on extroverted intuition, our mental equilibrium is threatened. We may become excited by multiple new opportunities but lack the follow-through to actually commit to any of them. We enter the 'danger zone' where we're at risk of jumping from one new idea or plan to the next to the next, scouring our money and health and resources in the process.

Extroverted intuition also works as a powerful distractor. If we are not ready to deal with the emotional impact of what we are going through, Ne may set up arbitrary challenges to distract us. In this case, we are in danger of falling into a dominant-tertiary loop (this will be covered in greater detail in following chapters).

After an extended period of time dwelling in extroverted intuition, the ENFP will feel drained on a physical, mental and emotional level. By this point they will likely have begun and terminated various new projects, depleted their resources on multiple levels and exhausted the majority of their options. If they have not found the answer that they are looking for to the problem at hand, the ENFP will be forced to move past their extroverted intuition in search of a solution to their problem – and pass the reigns onto their introverted feeling.

Personal Interlude: Extroverted Intuition Fails

After graduating University, I planned to move to South Korea for a year to teach English. I secured a job with the Korean government – set to begin in September – and headed off to work my pre-arranged summer job. While working on my summer assignment, I received word that I'd been bumped onto a 'Wait list' for the teaching position in South Korea, as they'd over-hired.

'No worries!' My extroverted intuition encouraged. 'We'll just find another job. It'll be fun!'

Night after night, I came home from work and scoured the TEFL boards. I eventually found a position of interest in Taiwan, interviewed for it and was hired over Skype. I was a little stressed about the whole situation – the school in Taiwan didn't seem particularly reputable but hey, it was something to do.

'Don't worry!' My extroverted intuition encouraged, 'We'll distract ourselves with a fun vacation before going to Taiwan.'

So I got online that evening and booked a plane ticket to Thailand.

Immediately upon arriving in Thailand, everything about my decision seemed off. I got sent my contract for the Taiwan job and found a few holes in it, to say the least. The food in Thailand was another point of contention – everything seemed to be cross contaminated with shellfish, which I was allergic to, and I spent the first week doubled over a toilet in my hostel, growing steadily more delirious with each day I lay sick in the sweltering heat.

'Don't worry!' My extroverted intuition chimed in. 'Why don't you ditch the job and fly home? You have an apartment in Canada with your boyfriend, he'll be happy to have you back.'

So I cabbed to the airport that evening and flew the whole thirty hours home.

Upon arriving back in Canada, my overwhelmed boyfriend broke up with me. 'You can't just keep coming and going like this,' he accused. And that seemed to make sense. I packed up my part of the apartment and returned to the airport feeling plan-less.

'Don't worry!' Chimed my extroverted intuition. 'Your best friend just moved to the West coast. We'll fly out to visit her for a while. It'll be fun!'

And so out West I went. I crashed with my best friend for a

few weeks and found that the West Coast suited me – but my depleted bank account did not.

'We'll find a job!' My Ne suggested. 'And an apartment! A whole new city and a challenging new career, what fun!'

And so that's what I did. I found a place to live, a place to work, a few friends to hang out with and a gym to join. Once those things were set in place, my extrovert packed its bags and gave the hell up on me.

'Have fun!' Said my extroverted intuition. 'You've exhausted me and I am OUTTA HERE.'

Stage 2: Introverted Feeling Fails

Introverted feeling is the ENFP's executive assistant. Extroverted intuition is constantly compiling new experiences, new challenges and new events – all of which it dumps in a pile on Introverted Feeling's desk and says, "Sort through this."

Luckily, introverted feeling loves its job.

Introverted feeling has a huge corner office in the ENFP's brain where it regularly holes itself up, shuts the blinds and festers for days at a time. It categorizes ideas into boxes labeled either, "Yes, let's!" Or "No way in hell." It categorizes moral quandaries into folders labeled, "Right" or "Wrong" or "Needs further clarification: Return to Extroverted Intuition for additional input." It occasionally sits on a particular experience for ages, flipping it over in its hands and trying to rearrange it into something entirely new. Fi can be a procrastinator at large, but it always gets the job done eventually.

Introverted feeling may not be our dominant function but it is, in essence, the neck that turns Ne's head. No decision gets made without Fi giving the go-ahead. Fi is happy being second-in-command but when Ne goes on vacation, Fi has to run the whole office. And quite frankly, it is not a great boss.

When Ne packs up and leaves, Fi's plan of attack is basically, "Okay, we'll just sort through what we have until Extroverted Intuition comes back." And so it retreats into its office labeled "Introspection."

When an ENFP runs out of ideas, introspection becomes a fixation point. We go home, shut the blinds, turn the music on and tell ourselves we're going to think our way out of the hole we've gotten into. No longer relying on extroverted intuition, we lose our regular 'sparkle' and feel incapable and unconfident. We don't want the world to see us at our worst and so we hide from the world. We tell ourselves that by sitting with our feelings and sorting through what's going on internally, we can reach the conclusion we need.

Sometimes this works. Sometimes the ENFP simply does need a bout of introspection to help them connect with what's going on externally. Other times, however, Introverted Feeling isn't ready to solve its own problems – and so it distracts itself with busywork. It calls up the Introverted Sensing department and says, "Please send over all of the documents I failed to categorize over the past five years."

Next thing you know, Fi is rooting through a box labeled, "My dinner party from 2010," and filing, "That comment my mother-in-law made about my baby weight," under, "Anger." It is no surprise that at this phase, the ENFP may begin lashing out at others in a seemingly unpredictable fashion.

In extreme circumstances, Fi may attempt to masquerade as an extroverted function – assuming it can accomplish all that Extroverted Intuition can. This can quickly turn into a disaster. Over-exerted introverted feeling attempts to analyze and categorize the feelings of everyone around the ENFP – ignoring its own responsibilities by assuming the responsibilities of everyone else. It takes on the problems of loved ones as though they are its own problems and secretly hopes for validation and recognition for all that it is doing.

The problem with this situation is that while Fi believes it is acting as a rock for others, it is actually hopelessly dependent on those others benefiting from its contributions. Fi is unknowingly desperate for validation and it is willing to overtax itself as much as necessary to receive it. This is an unhealthy spiral for everyone involved and can severely harm the ENFP's close relationships. The ENFP may grow angry with those around them for resisting their advice or failing to appreciate their help. Introverted Feeling truly does believe that it is doing good work and ought to be appreciated, at this phase. This lack of self-awareness is, ironically, a key indicator of unhealthy Fi.

Personal Interlude: Introverted Feeling Fails

When I arrived on the West Coast and moved in with my best friend, things were great – for a while. I went out with new friends, settled into my new job and began to build a life in the new city.

And yet, something was off. I had that nagging feeling ENFPs tend to experience when they know that they've left something emotionally unprocessed. But I didn't particularly want to process my personal or professional failures, so I resolutely ignored them. For a short period of time I fell into a dominant-tertiary loop and when that was over, I reluctantly resigned to my Introverted Feeling.

"Okay Introverted Feeling," I said (being an introvert, Fi almost never starts the conversation itself), "What can we work on that has absolutely nothing to do with me?"

And so Introverted Feeling shyly pointed its fingers at a couple of my friends from back home who were experiencing personal difficulties. And I ran at those difficulties full force.

For the following few months, my life became consumed by the struggles of my loved ones. I spent hours on Skype with them. I woke up in the middle of the night to answer texts from them. I lamented and agonized and pained over their problems as though they were my own, because, in a way, they were. I wrapped myself up in their struggles so tightly that they became a part of who I was. I wouldn't be happy until they were, I decided. Solving their problems was my mission and I'd be happy again once I'd completed it.

But here's the problem with taking on someone else's difficulties as your own: It creates a toxic situation for all parties. My friends were dependent on my emotional support and I was dependent on their validation that I was a good, worthwhile person. My Fi had no input from Ne to confirm this on its own so it relied on other people to provide it. I was only as good as I was helpful and I was only as helpful as my friends were successful.

And so I helped and I helped and I helped – until Fi absolutely exhausted itself. It began filing every conversation under "Miserable," and every problem under "Hopeless." It's not that it thought my friends' issues themselves were hopeless – rather that I felt hopeless to process their problems and inspire a solution. Introverted feeling was tired of behaving as my dominant function and exerting itself in unnatural ways.

So one morning I woke up and found a note pasted to Introverted Feeling's door. "Joining Ne on vacation," It said. "Extroverted Thinking will take the reigns from here."

Stage 3: Extroverted Thinking Fails

In terms of its place within the ENFP's brain, Extroverted Thinking is the hotshot personal assistant who went to Harvard and got straight A's but somehow couldn't score that coveted job leading the ENTJ to victory, so it ended up as Introverted Feeling's personal assistant in the ENFP's brain instead. Sometimes Te's kind of pissed that it's the most competent employee in the office with the second most meaningless job, but nobody else really cares or listens to Te when it complains. Over time, it's learned to work alongside Fi quite well and has forgotten that it ever once had bigger dreams.

Te takes the input that Fi gives it – the folders labeled,

"Yes, let's!" Or "Hell No," and implements whichever plans need to be implemented. If "A trip to Indonesia," is what is inside the "Yes, let's!" folder, Extroverted Thinking goes online and books the ticket. If "Discriminating against gay people" is in the "Hell no!" folder, Te steps up to bat and argues about equal rights with the ENFP's prejudiced Uncle over Thanksgiving Dinner. Te is diligent and dedicated to its job, even though it took Introverted Feeling about thirty years to actually acknowledge Te as an employee.

Anyway. When Ne and Fi pack up and go on vacation together, Te gets the chance to run the office at last. It takes the last of Fi's recent commands and does whatever it can to apply them to the ENFP's life. If the last thing Fi wanted before it left was to excel at work, Te pours itself into work – it commands the ENFP to pull twelve hour days and work like an absolute dog. Te does whatever it can think of to pull itself out of the state of stagnancy that Fi's leadership induced.

At this stage of their downward spiral, the ENFP will be desperately attempting to implement structure into their lives. Having moved past the over-reliance on their introverted feeling, they will likely realize that they have let their external environments grow stagnant and will attempt to rectify matters by setting concrete goals for themselves. They may schedule plans with friends, search for a new job or begin a personal development project that will bring them closer to the person they want to be. They may feel somewhat numb while carrying out all these activities, but nonetheless be quietly confident that if their goals come to fruition, they will feel happy once again.

At this stage, the ENFP may turn their situation around.

Re-engaging with their tertiary extroverted function may also re-engage their neglected extroverted intuition (as the more time they spend engaging with the outer world, the more their dominant extroverted function sees the chance to jump in) and filter new input through the introverted feeling in a healthy manner. If, however, the plans and goals that the ENFP sets at this stage are unsuccessful, they are at risk of falling into the clasp of their inferior function, and watching their shadow functions manifest.

Personal Interlude: Extroverted Thinking Fails

After several months out West, I realized things were not working for me. I'd eased communication with my struggling friends from back home, but was brutally aware that I was now facing struggles of my own. I was barely making enough money to cover rent, which put me in a perpetual state of inaction. I couldn't go out, couldn't socialize, couldn't splurge – ever – and couldn't even cover a gym membership. I felt sluggish, unfulfilled and depressed.

So my Te kicked in. Surveying the situation, it told me it was time to both revamp my schedule and find another job. Instead of working long, unpaid hours to distract myself from my dissatisfying personal life, I started leaving work on time and coming home to apply for new opportunities. Every evening I'd apply to something new. Every morning, I'd wake up two hours earlier than usual and write.

Writing was my passion – it always had been – and my dream was to make a living out crafting words. I wasn't feeling particularly creative at that point in my life, so I wrote technical articles. I wrote about Myers-Briggs. I wrote about being stuck. I wrote how-to's and listicles and weary attempts at self-help guides. I wrote what I knew – feeling certain that my creativity would return to me once my conditions began looking up.

Eventually, things did. It took months of following my own regimented plans for things to start turning around but in the meantime, my extroverted thinking began to lose confidence. It implemented its order and then just waited.

And while it was waiting, introverted sensing took over.

Stage 4: Introverted Sensing Takes Over

Introverted Sensing is a huge filing room full of little minions who run around and place experiences into pre-categorized shelves based on which observations Extroverted Intuition hands down to them and how Introverted Feeling and Extroverted Thinking suggest they be filed.

This system works quite effectively in an ISxJ's brain because the minions are granted full autonomy to organize and create structure as they see fit. In an ENFP brain, however, the filing room is chaos because just as the minions are finally starting to get things organized, Ne has the habit of bursting into the filing room, throwing piles of uncategorized papers all over the floor, laughing maniacally and then leaving. Some things simply never get sorted.

Si is very rarely given autonomy in the ENFP brain. Even

when it does chime in from time to time – suggesting a healthier diet or a consistent work schedule to the other functions, Ne is quick to shut it down.

"I HAVE A FUNNER IDEA," Ne will yell, and Fi will file the fun new idea under "Yes, let's!" And then Introverted Sensing will retreat to its file room in shame.

Understandably, Si isn't the ENFP's most confident function. When it lacks direction or instruction from the first three functions, it second-guesses itself and files almost everything that happens under "DANGER!"

And in the clasp of their inferior function, this is exactly what the ENFP does.

An unhealthy ENFP – one who has fallen all the way through their stacking to rest on their introverted sensing as a primary mode of processing information – becomes regimented, paranoid and anxious. They perceive negative possibilities at every turn and become too scared to make a significant move in any direction.

The unhealthy ENFP may become compulsive about maintaining whatever form of order they have implemented over their lives. They may obsess over details that they'd normally dismiss without a second thought and cling to routines or behaviors that do not necessarily serve them.

Manifestation Of The Shadow Functions

When Introverted Sensing takes over, the ENFP's functions work in reverse order – Si feeds into Ne, rather than the other way around, and Te dictates Fi. Their reversed function stacking makes them resemble their dichotomous four-letter opposite, the ISTJ. However, the ENFP's under-exercised Si does not function with the capability and balance that the ISTJ's dominant Si does – they will therefore behave as an unhealthy or imbalanced ISTJ.

The ENFP may lose faith on their ability to change the future in this state, as their introverted sensing blows their present circumstances out of proportion and projects into their extroverted intuition. When they look towards the future, the ENFP will envision all of the ways in which their present circumstances could continue on and manifest negatively (Quenk, 2002). If they are stressed about work, they will envision a series of negative developments that could manifest in the workplace, making their situation worse. If they are lonely, they will mentally prepare themselves for further abandonment by those they care about – convincing themselves that this is likely to happen. The ENFP may feel helpless to stop these negative projections, as they have become hopelessly out of touch with their extroverted intuition as a stand-alone function.

When the ENFP's shadow functions are at play, introverted sensing is also likely to manifest as anxiety over bodily functions (Quenk, 2002). ENFPs tend to be somewhat out of touch with their bodies under normal circumstances and they may fail to notice the little twinges or pains that regularly occur throughout the course of a day. When they are in the clasp of their shadow functions, however, ENFPs are hyper-tuned to these twinges and pains. They may experience a great deal of anxiety in relation to them, believing a momentary spell of dizziness to be indicative of a brain tumor or an isolated chest pang to tell the tale of an impending heart attack. Their introverted sensing is, once again, projecting into their extroverted intuition and assigning a big-picture problem to a momentary sensation.

Since their functions are working in reverse order in this state, the ENFP's extroverted thinking will dictate their interactions with others and dominate introverted feeling. Rather than coming across as their bubbly, optimistic selves, the ENFP will be curt and formal in their interactions with others – discussing things in a matter-of-fact fashion and convincing even themselves that they will be happy again once they've accomplished their goals.

Though the ENFP often wishes under regular circumstances that their feelings would take a backseat to their logic, it's important to remember that during shadow function manifestation, the ENFP's extroverted thinking is not functioning in a healthy manner. Their logic may be skewed and irrational, or it may be a constantly moving point. They may decide that they'll be happy once they lose ten pounds, only to lose ten pounds and decide they'll be happy after another five.

An ENFP using their shadow functions is an anxious, irrational ENFP who may ironically believe that they are behaving more practically and logically than ever. What will urge them out of this state, however, is the lack of fulfillment and pervasive state of unhappiness that they experience when they stay trapped within it for an extend period of time.

Personal Interlude: Shadow Functions Activated

The longer I spent out West, the more control I exerted over my life.

From an outside perspective, this may have looked like a positive development. I was routine-oriented. I was productive. I was budget-conscious to a borderline obsessive extent. Internally, however, I was falling apart.

I became certain that someone I loved was going to die. It wasn't the most paranoid delusion out there, as I did have a couple of loved ones in particularly ill health at the time. But the idea consumed my thoughts. I kept a constant check on the prices of plane tickets to their respective cities, should I have to pick up and go for their funerals. I sent an obsessive amount of text messages. I woke up several times each night to make sure I hadn't missed an ominous phone call from a loved one's family member.

Beyond that, I became obsessive about my own health. Several times a day I convinced myself that I, too, was dying. A new mole was skin cancer. A spell of dizziness was an impending stroke. I became so consumed with the idea that I was going to have a heart attack that I would routinely check my own pulse for upsets or irregularities.

Negative perceptions had taken over my life and the idea that my situation would ever come to an end was implausible. I was convinced that not only would I never get a new job, make enough money to live off or see my loved ones return to health, but I was positive that things would continue to spiral. My job performance would fall, I would get fired, a loved one would die, and then I would die too. This is what my introverted sensing was telling me, on a steady, never-ending loop. And it was exhausting.

Introverted sensing was taking care of me in some respects – it kept me to my schedule of going to work, applying for new jobs, and writing for hours every morning. It managed my money, paid my bills and kept me eating a healthy diet. But it was an abusive caretaker – one that would encourage and then belittle me. I had no idea how to properly manage my introverted sensing, so I took it at face value. It told me I had dying loved ones, heart issues and no hope for the future and I believed it. After all, that's what you do when you're down on your luck – you believe in absolutely anything that happens to be keeping you afloat.

13

Moving Out Of The Shadows

The end goal of escaping from one's shadow is to re-engage your dominant function and return your function stacking to its natural order. However, a direct re-engagement of extroverted intuition is not always possible for the ENFP who has been operating from their introverted sensing for a significant period of time, as they will have adopted the habit of using their extroverted intuition to project negative possibilities onto their future. Consequently, the ENFP may have to return to their extroverted intuition by moving backwards through their cognitive stacking, engaging each function in a deliberately healthy fashion as they go.

This process begins with introverted sensing. Simply put, the ENFP needs to take back control of their file room and stop filing everything under "DANGER." This may take time, patience and persistence. Particularly if they are in their younger years, the ENFP is likely to have neglected their introverted sensing for the majority of their lives, as this function doesn't fully develop until approximately middle age. Until then, the ENFP has to be deliberate and purposeful about engaging their Si.

Engaging introverted sensing in a healthy manner means:

- Getting a strict eight hours of sleep each night.
- Engaging in consistent, regular exercise.
- Eating a healthy, balanced diet.
- Spending a minimum of thirty minutes per day outdoors, in the sunlight (if possible).
- Showering and putting on presentable attire every morning (regardless of whether or not you'll be leaving the house).
- Visiting the doctor to address any health concerns (or lack thereof).
- Maintaining a regular, predictable schedule that your body can physically adjust to for a minimum of one month.

These lifestyle adjustments may seem laughably obvious to other types – but for the ENFP, they are a stark contrast to their usual way of living. In fact, an ENFP reading this is likely to scoff at the simplicity of these suggestions and assume that there must be a psychological short cut they can take to launch themselves out of the grip of their shadow functions should they ever find themselves there. This is a prime example of our tendency as ENFPs to believe that we are mentally above our physical needs. Unfortunately, we are not. And we need to engage those needs positively in order to return to mental equilibrium.

The positive engagement of introverted sensing (over a period of weeks or months) provides a sense of external structure for the ENFP, which is psychologically soothing to them. The minions in the file room of introverted sensing will slowly, systematically cease to file everything under "DANGER," and the ENFP will begin feeling safe to re-engage their other functions in a positive manner. Their next step will likely be to re-engage their extroverted thinking.

Engaging extroverted thinking in a healthy manner means:

- Stepping back to objectively evaluate how you are doing physically, financially, professionally, socially, mentally and emotionally.
- Determining any discrepancies that exist between where you currently are and where you'd like to be.
- Setting specific, measurable goals that will help you diminish those discrepancies.
- Taking consistent, deliberate action to work toward said goals.
- Consistently re-evaluating where you are in relation to your goals and re-assessing your plan of attack as necessary.

Since functions work in pairs, extroverted thinking bleeds into introverted feeling, even in an unhealthy state. Your hopes and ideals are likely to emerge through the goals you set and this is a positive thing – it means your introverted feeling is stepping up to bat and asking for the chance to re-emerge. The more your extroverted thinking develops, the more comfortable you may begin to feel accessing your emotions and allowing feeling back into your everyday life.

Engaging introverted feeling in a healthy manner means:

- Allowing yourself to emotionally process both positive and negative emotions as they arise.
- Reaching out to loved ones to repair (or end) damaged relationships.
- Opening yourself up to others about the struggles you've been encountering and accepting emotional support.
- Reconnecting with the creative/artistic side of your personality.
- Allowing yourself permission to feel sadness, love, despair, hope and a plethora of other emotions as they arise.
- Reconnecting with your values and ideals – and, with the help of extroverted thinking, taking definitive action to work toward your vision of a better, more authentic 'you.'

Once their introverted feeling has been re-engaged in a positive manner, the ENFP is likely to naturally reconnect with their extroverted intuition. They will once again feel comfortable brainstorming new ideas, taking on new challenges and speculating about all of the possibilities that exist for their future. Having strengthened their inferior, tertiary and auxiliary functions in the process of returning to health, the ENFP may actually see a stronger, more well-rounded version of extroverted intuition when it re-emerges – one that can apply judgment and follow-through to its many perceptions.

Extroverted intuition working in cooperation with the other functions means:

- Balancing perceptions with judgments and decisions.
- Taking one's physical and emotional needs into account when brainstorming future opportunities.
- Possessing the ability to convey new ideas in a clear and concise manner.
- Having the persistence and execution to follow new ideas through to fruition.

Of course, a single shadow experience is unlikely to self-actualize an ENFP to the point where he or she never places an over-reliance on a single function again. But the process of moving through each function in their return to health can be surprisingly beneficial for the ENFP in the long term.

Personal Interlude: Returning To Health

After many months out West, my physical health began to deteriorate. I began experiencing extreme stomach pains that forced me to stay home from work for weeks at a time and confirmed my hypothesis that I was, in fact, dying. I finally brought myself to the hospital, braced for the news that one of the ominous health conditions I'd Googled was finally getting the best of me.

I was surprised to be released from the hospital shortly afterwards with the news that my stomach pains were a product of severe indigestion, brought on by stress.

"But I'm not stressed," I remember explaining to the doctor in a panic. "I have everything under control. It must be a blood clot. Or stomach cancer."

Luckily, my doctor was a boss bitch who wasn't having any of my shit. "You are fine," She replied dismissively. "You will just learn to manage your anxiety."

Granted, this was easier said than done. But learning that my ill health was self-induced did serve as a definitive turning point.

Over the next few weeks, I paid particular attention to my physical health. I ate healthily, made time to exercise and continued adhering to a strict daily schedule. I kept applying to jobs at night and writing one article each morning. I wasn't sure if anything would come of it, but it was all I could think to keep doing.

One day, I finally received a phone call (okay, an email) from a major publication – they were hiring, and my application had caught their eye! They wanted me to join their team as a writer.

At any other time in my life, I would have been overjoyed. My dream of making a living as a writer was going to come true! And yet, I felt nothing. I'd become so detached from my introverted feeling that even my dream job landing in my lap didn't induce the sense of joy that once came so easily to me. But it did bring me the opportunity for a change – which activated my extroverted thinking.

Over the next few weeks, I got busy packing my life up to move back East. The new-found opportunity to work from anywhere allowed me the freedom to relocate to somewhere where the rent was cheap, my community was plentiful and the rain was not constantly falling from the sky. I got myself set up in a new apartment – one that I could actually afford – reconnected with old friends and set concrete goals for myself to work toward professionally. Things made sense again. I was beginning to trust myself, after a prolonged period of making only mistakes.

One spring morning, a few weeks after moving back East, I found myself walking through my old neighborhood. As I passed by the street-level apartment I'd once shared with my ex-partner, the door opened – and a middle-aged man in a business suit walked out.

The emergence of a stranger from the apartment that I'd once moved into with so much hope and excitement caught me completely off guard. In a single heartbreaking moment, every feeling I'd been repressing for the better part of a year about my breakup came rushing at me full force. I barely made it home before completely breaking down into tears. And once the tears came, they didn't stop.

That afternoon I cried over my ex. I cried over losing my job abroad. I cried over the loved ones I couldn't help and the new beginning I'd failed at so massively. I cried because I was scared I'd mess up at my new job. I cried for everything I'd messed up in the past.

And the cool thing about all that crying was that by the time the tears subsided and the sun began to sink in the sky, I felt different. Calmer. Humbler. More at peace than I'd felt in a good year since I'd left the same city I was back in.

And from that day onward, things felt different. Happiness started returning to me, slowly but surely. I felt proud of my professional advances. Excited about upcoming projects.

Joyful to be in the presence of old loved ones and new friends – even on the days when joy came mixed with a painful nostalgia. And the more space I allowed myself to heal, the more excited I became about the future.

My extroverted intuition returned naturally as I allowed my introverted feeling to breathe. I began to plan trips, projects, getaways and developments. My dreams for the future ran wild – I became fearlessly perceptive of what could happen next and ways in which I could progress professionally.

Only this time, the perceptions of the future were infused with a distinct element of realism – I understood that I'd need to look a little more carefully before leaping in the future. And I was grateful for the knowledge that realism provided – I knew I could handle what came next. After all, I'd come back from the worst.

The Benefits Of Shadow Experiences

While reverting to one's shadow functions is anything but a

pleasant experience, it can be a highly actualizing one for any type. The process of returning to health by re-engaging each function in a healthy manner helps the ENFP to understand precisely what they need to stay balanced on a physical, emotional and intellectual level. Rather than allowing their extroverted intuition to run wild (as younger ENFPs are particularly prone to doing), the ENFP will come to understand how a healthy balance of each cognitive function can help them to thrive.

Shadow experiences remind us of the importance of staying balanced throughout periods of good health, so that periods of ill health do not leave us defenseless. Though extroverted intuition and introverted sensing do not fully develop in ENFPs until adulthood, the young ENFP can nonetheless learn to consciously engage them when needed in order to stay healthy, balanced and productive.

14

Dominant-Tertiary Loops

The manifestation of shadow functions is not the only possible reaction the ENFP can have to periods of extreme stress.

A dominant-tertiary loop occurs when an individual of any type switches to dwelling exclusively in the social realm they are most comfortable in – that is, extroversion for extroverts and introversion for introverts. They will neglect the input of their auxiliary function and move directly from their dominant function to their tertiary one while taking in new information and making decisions. This leads to a temporary (or in some cases pervasive) imbalance in personality – introverted types fail to interact with the outside world, whereas extroverted types lose touch with their inner world.

Despite the fact that ENFPs are the most introverted extroverts, they are ultimately more comfortable dwelling in the realm of ideas and possibilities than they are in the realm of feelings and sentiments. They consider their emotions to be highly private and even what they do share with the outside world is often a careful orchestration of how they would like to be perceived. ENFPs are not naturally emotionally expressive when it comes to what they feel deep down – but they are naturally in touch with those emotions. They just require a great deal of alone time to process and reflect on them.

A dominant-tertiary loop occurs when an ENFP ceases to consult their introverted feeling function and moves directly from their extroverted intuition to their extroverted thinking. It's important to note here that deliberately neglecting one's auxiliary function in a specific situation (i.e. leaving one's feelings out of a decision in the workplace) is not considered a loop. Loops primarily develop as the result of some emotional trauma or upset that the ENFP feels unable to process. Rather than confront the negative emotions head-on, they will turn to distracting themselves via the outer world of possibilities and challenges – and will oftentimes be unaware that they are even doing so.

A dominant-tertiary loop in an ENFP is likely to manifest in one or more of the following ways:

1. Becoming goal-oriented to a fault.

ENFPs are naturally goal-oriented. However, a loop may manifest as a pattern of setting and accomplishing goals in a rapid-fire way, without pause to evaluate the significance or meaning of said goals. This may seem productive on a surface level, but the truth is, these goals are almost always shallow and geared towards acquiring recognition. Because the ENFP has become over-reliant on the external realm, they will become dependent on impressing others with their success and they will only ever be as happy as they are admired.

The type of goals the ENFP sets may in part depend on Enneagram type. A Type 7 ENFP may aspire to visit several countries or states in quick succession, documenting their travels as they go and reaping recognition through digital comments and 'likes.' A type 4 ENFP may mass-promote their creative endeavors and demand excessive amounts of recognition for their work. A type 2 ENFP may throw themselves into organizing a charity event or helping out a loved one, and then expect endless amounts of praise for their selflessness.

2. Developing an over-reliance on feedback or praise.

An ENFP in a dominant-tertiary loop has few means of defining themselves on a personal level, so they will turn to others to affirm and validate them. They may become uncharacteristically boastful – demanding recognition for their accomplishments, or even guilt tripping loved ones by claiming that they do not appreciate all the ENFP does for them.

They will want to spend as little time as possible alone, and will constantly be on their friends' case to hang out with them or go socializing – if their friends aren't as available as they'd like, they'll likely expand their social circle. The ENFP will constantly surround themselves with others, in order to distract themselves from their internal world.

3. Becoming uncharacteristically hostile and/or argumentative.

An ENFP in a dominant-tertiary loop will oscillate quickly between their idea-generating function and their reasoning function – meaning they will become masters of explaining away their newest endeavor and will be wholly uninterested in receiving contrary feedback. They may lose their usual sense of compassion and snap back at those who question them, shutting their arguments down with indisputable logic. They will become unconcerned with the interpersonal consequences of their action and may seem uncharacteristically cold or detached in their reasoning.

4. Placing blame on others.

Since an ENFP in a dominant-tertiary loop lacks the ability to introspect, they will attribute any problems they may face to their external environment. This becomes particularly problematic in the realm of interpersonal relationships. An ENFP in a dominant-tertiary loop is at risk of becoming highly manipulative, as their Ne points out opportunities to sway others for their own gain and their Te is quick to implement those strategies. The unhealthy ENFP may guilt, gaslight or even coerce others into behaving in a way that benefits them personally. They will likely feel little remorse for their actions, as an ENFP in a loop may truly believe that other people are the root of their problems.

5. Engaging in excessive sensation-seeking.

The longer an ENFP goes without pulling themselves out of a loop, the more extreme their actions will become as they search for sources of external stimulation. They may turn to excessive drug or alcohol consumption, engage in risky sexual behavior or spend money lavishly. They will be constantly searching for the next 'high,' and will use their Te to explain away their outlandish actions to both others and themselves.

ENFPs Share Their Experiences In Dominant-Tertiary Loops

"After the death of my mother I went into a dominant-tertiary loop. I couldn't handle losing her so I became obsessive about getting fit as a distraction. I joined three different fitness classes and I rotated between them. I lost almost twenty pounds and liked the way I looked so then I upped my goal and decided I needed to get toned, too. I remember my husband telling me I was getting obsessive and needed to ease up on the workouts but I had no interest in doing so. I snapped at him and told him he wasn't disciplined like me. Eventually I wore myself to the ground and realized it was time to stop working out so much and start facing reality. But it took a while. I really didn't want to spend time inside my head at that point in my life."
-Kelsey, 43

"When I was twenty-one my first serious boyfriend cheated on me and then left me for the other woman and I totally flew off the handle. This is embarrassing but I really needed validation and so I set sex goals for myself. Like, I made a list of people I wanted to get with and pursued each one of them until I slept with them. It made me feel cool and like I was in control and nothing could hurt me but after a while I just started to feel empty. I realized I was a lot sadder than I was letting myself believe about losing my ex. And I had to actually let myself be sad about that instead of just trying to move on with all these other people."

-Angie, 25

"When I got my first full-time job after college, it went to my head big-time. I was doing investment banking (weird career for an ENFP, I know) and the guys in my office were really competitive and I wanted to prove myself – so I just started working ALL the time. I took on work that I definitely didn't have time to do but just kept thinking about the next project and then the next one. I also stopped hanging out with anyone except the other junior bankers because we were always at the office – and they were kind of dicks so I never used my feeling side around them. Eventually my girlfriend (who I was living with) broke up with me because I was never at home and I was grumpy and cold around her even when I was. That was my wake-up call that I needed to change something."

-Liam, 29

Escaping The Loop

To escape from a dominant-tertiary loop, the ENFP needs to re-engage their introverted feeling. This function acts as a mediator between their dominant and tertiary functions, allowing them to balance out extroverted intuition's crazy ideas with introspective personal judgments.

An ENFP usually enters a loop due to an external trauma or upset that they do not feel capable of emotionally processing. Therefore, the following methods may help an ENFP escape their loop:

1. Seeking professional help. If the upset they are facing is too severe for the ENFP to process alone, they may benefit immensely from seeking the help of a professional. A doctor, therapist or psychiatrist may be able to tap into the ENFP's emotional reserves and help them process the upset they are facing in a safe and controlled environment.

2. Structuring "Introverted Feeling Time." An ENFP in a loop is more trustful of their extroverted thinking than they are of their introverted feeling – and they can use this to their advantage. They can use their extroverted thinking to structure alone time and plan safe environments within which they can process their feelings.

For example, an ENFP who recognizes that they are stuck in a loop may schedule one hour per day for yoga, meditation or deliberate introspection. By keeping their 'Fi time' regimented, they can ease the anxiety that they will fall down the rabbit hole of their emotions if they begin to explore them.

The more time they spend alone in a safe and controlled environment, the more they will begin to trust their introverted processes – and the more accessible their introverted feeling will become.

3. Learning to consciously acknowledge negative feelings. ENFPs are eternal optimists – they see the good in every situation and as a result, often have trouble processing experiences that they cannot put a positive spin on. Many loops develop as an ENFP's method of 'escaping' a negative situation or feeling that their minds do not want to accept.

In order to move past these types of loops, the ENFP must find a way to accept and process their negative emotions, without immediately allowing their extroverted intuition to hop in and save the day. How they do so will be different for every ENFP – some may turn to journaling as a method of releasing negative emotions, some may speak with a close friend, others may simply let themselves cry and wallow for a short period of time, until the pain subsides.

Regardless of their method of coping, the ENFP must find a way to process all feelings that come their way – the good, the bad and the downright excruciating – if they want to avoid lapsing back into a dominant-tertiary loop in the future.

15

Managing Your Moods

Even when all functions are operating in the correct order, ENFPs are extremely moody creatures.

In many ways, our type is perpetually childlike. Our emotions are intense and volatile and we think that we're the masters of our own Universe. That we don't need what other people need. That we can work all day and play all night and be fine, because we are not like other people.

But we're wrong. Like children, we are not the superheroes we wish we were. We need strong, firm adults in our lives. And that those adults have to be us.

When we feel as though we're coming undone, the ENFP's natural inclination is to ride the wave of our feelings – indulging in the negatives and enthusing over the positives. We exist in a perpetual state of highs and lows – and what we need to learn to do is stay peacefully on middle ground. We use the excuse that we never *feel* that middle ground – it simply doesn't come naturally to us. And that's true. It doesn't come naturally to us. But we can deliberately create it.

Intuitives need to be extremely deliberate about taking care of themselves. To sensing types, this comes naturally. Hunger means eat, exhaustion means sleep and loneliness means go out and socialize. We, however, are not sensors. ENFPs are constantly looking for the hidden meaning behind everything

– to the point where we loathe accepting the simple fixes. We want our problems to have interesting, complex answers and so we cast aside the obvious ones.

It's unglamorous to admit that the majority of our struggles are born out of a simple lack of self-neglect. But they are. And if we truly want our moods to stabilize, we have to engage our extroverted thinking and introverted sensing to take concrete, definitive steps toward managing them.

Tracking Your Moods

As ENFPs, we often forget that our moods are largely dependent on our habits, behaviors and environments. By becoming conscious of which external stimulus corresponds to which of our moods, we can begin to organize our lives in a way that maximizes emotional stability.

The following exercise is designed to help you become aware of how your day-to-day habits impact your overall mood – and what you can do to ensure that the impact they have is a positive one.

Step 1:

Create a chart or agenda that separates each day of the week into approximately 2-hour blocks of time. For one week, record what you are doing at each point in time, as well as your mood on a scale of 1 (Depressed) – 5 (Elated).

Time	Activity	Mood
6-8am	Waking up and preparing for work day.	2
8am – 10am	At work – independent work.	3
10am – Noon	At work – meeting with clients.	4
Noon – 2pm	At work – filing reports.	1
2pm – 4pm	At work – working on a team project.	3
4pm – 6pm	Gym	3
6pm – 10pm	Dinner with friends or significant other	4
10pm – Midnight	Winding down/watching TV	3

Step 2:

Examine your chart for any patterns that emerge on both a daily basis and a weekly basis.

For example, within the scope of a single day, you may score 3 or higher every time you are surrounded by friends or loved ones. Conversely, perhaps you score 2 or lower every time you are doing a repetitive, detail-oriented task.

Also examine your chart for fluctuations based on certain activities over the scope of a week. For example, waking up and preparing for the workday may score 4 after a night of good sleep, but a 1 after a night of little sleep. You may notice that after the night of little sleep, the corresponding scores for the rest of your day are lower than usual.

Step 3:

Identify one area of potential improvement and alter your behavior accordingly for the corresponding week.

i.e. If you are consistently scoring 3 or higher when surrounded by people, add an additional hour of social time into your day, 3 days/week. Alternately, if you are consistently scoring 4 or higher between 6-8pm on the days when you exercise, head to the gym every day for a week.

Step 4:

Re-evaluate your mood chart after one week to see if your schedule alteration has had an impact on your overall mood. If possible, maintain the alteration for a minimum of a month to detect overall changes in wellbeing. If a particular activity shows an impact on your overall mood, consider adding it into your schedule as a permanent fixation.

Suggested alterations:

- Add an additional hour of sleep/night to your schedule
- Eat three balanced meals at specific times each day for a week
- Add 30 minutes of vigorous exercise to your schedule each day for a week
- Eat lunch with a friend or coworker every day for a week, if you usually eat it alone.
- Take one hour to journal at the end of each night for a week.

Why this exercise works:

This exercise plays on your extroverted thinking as a

measure of nurturing your introverted feeling. Rather than "Riding the wave" of your erratic emotions, you are learning to control and gently alter the wave – giving you a better sense of emotional regulation.

This exercise also highlights which introverted sensing habits you are and aren't engaging in healthily. It may bring a poor diet, exercise routine or sleep schedule to the forefront of your attention. Because we too often neglect our physical needs, ENFPs need to be deliberate about tracking and managing their habits.

16

Self-Care For ENFPs

On a day-to-day basis, ENFPs all seems to approach self-care a little differently.

Because this type has such varied interests, there seems to be no one-size-fits all solution for ENFPs who are feeling down – but there are a few commonalities that emerge. Most ENFPs report some interest in writing or journaling when they need to process their emotions. When it comes to a simple, inexplicable bad mood, most ENFPs report that spending time around loved ones picks them up – especially if they are engaging their extroverted intuition and making exciting plans with those loved ones.

I asked other ENFPs to weigh in on what they do to cheer themselves up when they're having a bad day – here is what they had to say!

"I encourage others, journal, read, or find something to celebrate!"

"I have drinks with friends – I need to surround myself with people and good energy. That or listening to songs and have a crying bout. I'm right as rain after that!"

"I volunteer or help someone else – or go do something fun (in public) where I have to act cheerful until I forget that I'm not."

"When I feel down I usually remember that a lot of people feel like that too and I jump online and share something funny with my followers to pick myself (and them) back up! Or I become pretty introverted and just recite songs or write lyrics."

"I run away from the crowd and think. Or I go to a friend and talk about it over and over until we figure out the answers."

"When I'm down I vent to someone I trust or go play sports and run all my angst out."

"I take a walk in a huge, populated park, chat with a friend, or go online and scroll through psychedelic pictures of plants for a while."

"When I feel down, I go to Costco to pick myself up! Something about walking around aimlessly in aisles and reading nutrition facts on food that just relaxes me."

"When I feel down, I ride motorbikes to pick myself back up! Not that I ever feel down though."

"When I feel down, I usually go on a trip or plan an adventure to somewhere I've never been, to do something I've never done – either with friends and family, or alone to meet new people."

"I am an ultra-sensitive empath who requires a lot of downtime for processing social interactions and renewing myself. For self-care, I rely on meditation, yoga, clean food, reading, listening to ambient trance music for hours alone at night, and long, luxurious baths with essential oils and DIY facial masks created from organic ingredients in my fridge, like Greek yogurt and raw honey."

"I go buy something and then dye my hair."

"I surround myself around with other people and talk to people, even if it's to go to the coffee shop and sit amongst the customers I don't even know. Energy from people recharges me."

"When I feel down I retreat into solitude and fantasy and make a world (with fae and without orcs)."

"I watch a movie I love and try to find the tiniest glimpse of a new idea or adventure to think about!"

"I tend to wander aimlessly outside in crowded areas to gain mental clarity – or just go to the gym."

"I have to receive a personal spiritual revelation to get perspective on my circumstances."

"When I'm down I like to dance. It's impossible to feel sad when dancing."

"When I feel down I hang out with friends, exercise, and read research articles to pick myself back up!"

"I need to do some "fangirling" and I need to start loving people again to pick myself back up!"

"Depending on the variety of down, I either steal people away on random adventures, and/or I induce a cuddle puddle with close friends."

"When down, I distract myself for a little while – if I still care in an hour or two, I evaluate what's wrong. Otherwise I know it was just another passing mood."

Part 5

ENFP Relationships

17

ENFPs As Friends

*"I don't care about whose DNA has recombined
with whose. When everything goes to hell, the
people who stand by you without flinching–they
are your family."*
–Jim Butcher

ENFPs take their friendships seriously.

Many ENFPs are raised in families that are predominantly made up of sensing types, and they may consequently find that their intuitive friends are the first people they've ever met who fully understand them and see them for who they truly are.

ENFPs bring an incredible amount of warmth, enthusiasm and love to their friendships. Though they're stereotyped as social butterflies, this type does not invest in all social relationships equally. The ENFP is likely to have a wide circle of people they're friendly with, but only a few people who know them on a deep level and whom they consider to be true, close friends.

The intensity, longevity and success of any friendship that the ENFP engages in will, of course, depend on the other party. Though ENFPs are capable of forming meaningful and long lasting friendships with any personality type, the nature of their relationship is likely to differ based on the temperament of the friend.

Soul Mates: NF Types

ENFPs tend to naturally form warm, long-lasting friendships with other intuitive, feeling types. These personalities (INFPs, INFJs, ENFJs and other ENFPs) share the ENFP's idealistic nature and are able to nurture them compassionately as they grow. These types are natural companions for the ENFP, who often feels instantly comfortable in their presence, knowing that they share a similar worldview and many of the same core values.

Complementary Opposites: NT Types

ENFPs tend to form challenging, stimulating friendships with intuitive thinking types. These personalities (INTJs, ENTJs, INTPs and ENTPs) challenge the ENFP's regular method of thinking and push them to grow intellectually. While these friendships may lack the warmth of their friendships with idealist types, ENFPs appreciate the ways in which their NT friends refuse to coddle them and instead push them to grow into better versions of themselves. These types are usually intrigued by one another upon first meeting and will likely recognize their intellectual connection quickly.

Partners In Crime: SP Types

ENFPs tend to form exciting, activity-based friendships with sensing, perceiving types. These personalities (ESFPs, ISFPs, ESTPs and ISTPs) are interested in experiencing life in full force and ENFPs tend to appreciate their shared enthusiasm for the world around them. These friendships are often short-lived or situation dependent, as they mainly revolve around shared experiences. However, ENFPs may experience a deeper or more long-lasting connection with ESFP and ISFP types, as they share their introverted feeling function and can connect on an emotional level.

Nurturing Opposites: SJ Types

ENFPs tend to form reliable, mutually respectful friendships with sensing, judging types. These personalities (ISFJs, ESFJs, ISTJs and ESTJs) provide a refreshing balance to the ENFP's erratic nature and may help bring them down to earth when the ENFP gets too caught up in the world of lofty ideals. Though they may experience some difficulty understanding one another intuitively, ENFPs tend to appreciate the stability and nurturance their SJ friends provide them with. In turn, SJ types appreciate the positive energy ENFPs bring to their lives. These relationships may be slow to form but are based on a strong sense of mutual respect.

18

ENFPs As Partners

"When I am with you, there is nowhere else I'd rather be. And I am a person who always wants to be somewhere else."
–David Levithan

ENFPs love love.

Warm, enthusiastic and affectionate, ENFPs make for truly dynamic lovers who are willing to go well out of their way to ensure that their relationship is a healthy and happy place for both partners to be.

Though they may be enthusiastic toward just about everyone they know, the ENFP possesses the unique ability to make their partner feel as though he or she is the only person in the world. This type throws themselves wholeheartedly into relationships and will do whatever is necessary to ensure that both partners are happy, healthy and growing together.

ENFPs are open-minded, explorative lovers who may engage in relationships with various different types over the course of their lives. Though any two types can certainly make it work, ENFPs tend to gravitate toward idealist and rational partners. Being an intuitive-dominant type, the ENFP tends to be drawn to other intuitive types for long-term partnership.

Those who lead with introverted intuition (INTJs and INFJs) are particularly well-suited for long-term partnership with the ENFP. We will explore those relationships in greater detail in the following chapter.

While ENFPs make for passionate, openhearted lovers, they often experience difficulty settling into a relationship that fulfills their own needs. This type needs a partner who can both challenge them and balance them out – and for the excitable ENFP, this can be a difficult combination to find!

What an ENFP Needs to be Happy in a Romantic Relationship

Growth

ENFPs are incredibly focused on personal growth. They enjoy taking on new challenges, pushing their limits and being immersed in a constant state of progression. And their relationships are no exception to this rule: ENFPs are constantly looking for ways to keep their relationships fresh and to grow together within them.

In order to stay satisfied long-term, the ENFP needs to know that they are with someone whom they can progress alongside. This type is best suited with a partner who also places a high value on self-improvement and who is constantly searching for ways to advance both individually and as a couple.

Stability

Though ENFPs tend to romanticize fiery, passionate love affairs with other spontaneous personalities, they are best suited for long-term relationships with partners who can provide them with a sense of stability and consistency. They may loathe admitting it, but ENFPs function best within structured environments. When a partner provides a sense of structure and emotional consistency for them, the ENFP is able to creatively flourish within the relationship. They can focus their enthusiasm on making the relationship a happy and exciting experience for both partners, rather than spending all of their energy just trying to keep it together.

Intellectual Stimulation

ENFPs may be hopeless romantics but they're intuitives first and foremost. This type craves a partnership that keeps them intellectually challenged and inspired in equal measure. Their version of romance is a late night debate that introduces them to a whole new way of looking at the world. This type is attracted to intelligence and they are best suited with a partner who shares their undying intellectual curiosity.

Variety

Though they require stability within their relationships, ENFPs loathe stagnancy. They want a relationship that opens them up to a variety of new experiences, challenges and thoughts. They are best suited with a partner who shares their enthusiasm for the world around them, as well as for the relationship itself. The ENFP is likely to come up with a steady stream of new ideas for keeping things fresh and exciting. If their partner is able to not just go along with them but also present new ideas of his or her own, the ENFP will be in seventh heaven.

Warmth and validation

ENFPs are highly affectionate people and they need to feel a sense of warmth and appreciation in return from their partner. When paired with thinking types who are not as openly affectionate as they are, ENFPs may go fishing for compliments or validation from their partners. They need to know that they are loved, cared for and appreciated – and they will always be the first to let their partners know the same.

Feeling free

As much as ENFPs love and appreciate the people in their lives, there is nothing more exciting to them than their latest idea – and they need a partner who understands that. This type stays in love for as long as they feel free alongside their partner – free to pursue their dreams, ideas and whims without restraint. They are best paired with a self-assured, independent individual, who isn't threatened by the ENFP's need to run off and explore on their own. At the end of the day, the ENFP always returns to whatever or whomever they love.

Warning to Other Types: Don't Date an ENFP

Don't date an ENFP. You'll never have the same day twice. ENFPs are a whirlwind of thoughts and plans. They are bursting with ideas of trips that you could take, of things you could create, of ways in which your lives could open up and expand and evolve. Monotony is not the ENFP cup of tea and they are constantly looking for ways to spice up life and keep things fresh. If you are looking for a dull, predictable partner who abhors trying anything new, you should run far from the ENFP.

Don't date an ENFP. They will challenge your opinions and thoughts. This type has a whirring, restless mind that examines things from every perspective. They will present you with new facts and figures. They'll entice you with new points of view. This type isn't one to sit back, nod politely and agree calmly with everything you say. ENFPs have a mind of their own and they will use it to invigorate yours. If it's a lifetime of small talk that you're looking for, steer clear of the ENFP.

Don't date an ENFP. They will shower you with love and affection. This type possesses a heart so full it's bursting –

with love for the people around them, with passion for their chosen career, with the world that they're lucky to live in and the people who make it all up. You will not wonder where you stand with an ENFP. They will flatter you with words and affection. They will rave about you to all their friends. They will readily remind you why they love you and they'll fight to ensure that you're happy. If you're looking for a cold and distant partner, the ENFP is not for you.

Don't date an ENFP. They'll show you what independence looks like. This type goes for what they want unabashedly and pursues each of their passions single-handedly. They will not fit into the palm of your hand; this type has wings that they intend to spread wide, they have goals and they intend to aim high. If you are looking for a quiet, docile partner, do not go after the ENFP. They don't expect a partnership to limit them and they don't plan to place limits on you either.

Don't date an ENFP. They will bring new people into your life. This type wants to hear everyone's stories – the server from the restaurant you frequent, the neighbor who waters their lawn six times a day, the man they met waiting at the bus stop. They will be best friends with your family within minutes. They'll infiltrate your friend group with ease. ENFPs love everybody they meet almost instantly and if you want a judgmental, standoffish, partner, the ENFP is not for you.

Don't date an ENFP. They'll push you to reach your full potential. They'll see the best in you, the brightest in you, the person you're capable of becoming, and they'll push you to become it. You'll never feel weak or incapable with the ENFP in your life. You'll have no excuse to sit back, wallow in a pool of self-pity and let your true potential pass you by. The ENFP will bring out the best in you. And if you're happy wallowing in your worst, you definitely shouldn't date one.

Don't date an ENFP. They will take you to go see the world. Life with the ENFP will be one big, never ending adventure. They'll cook you foods you've never tasted, bring you to places you've only dreamt of, sweep you away into a world full of excitement and passion and growth. Life will not be small or unremarkable with the ENFP by your side. There will be no room for playing it safe, for keeping it simple, for letting life pass you by one slow, monotonous day at a time.

You should not date an ENFP. Because they'll turn your whole world upside down. And you'll never be able to go back.

Common Relationship Challenges For ENFPs

ENFPs make for dynamic, engaged and enthusiastic partners. But that doesn't mean that every relationship they enter into is bound to be problem-free. ENFPs express difficulty in various areas when it comes to forming, staying in and leaving romantic relationships. Here are a few of the most common challenges ENFPs face in their love lives.

Committing to a new relationship

ENFPs tend to jump quickly into short-term relationships, but wade slowly and indecisively towards serious ones. They are the masters of keeping their options open and relationships are no exception to this rule. This type fears that by entering into a serious relationship they may be neglecting future possibilities for better partnerships. They may also miss the feeling of having all potential romantic options available to them. ENFPs hate feeling limited or restrained in any way and no matter how crazy they are about a particular person, some part of them is always going to see a serious relationship as a limiting factor.

How to work around it:

Paradoxically, ENFPs often have to arrive at a place where they feel comfortable making a decision by first thoroughly exploring the other possibilities that are available to them. They may choose to remain single for an extended period of time, explore various romantic options and spend years pursuing short-term relationships before they feel as though they have a good grasp on their options and are ready to decide on one long-term partner. Extroverted thinking develops through extensive usage of introverted feeling, so the more time the ENFP spends exploring their feelings, the more comfortable they will become discriminating between those options and applying judgment to their perceptions. It is important for the ENFP to remember that while dating around is fine, they need to be upfront and honest with potential partners about the fact that they're doing so. This type has the tendency to keep others in the dark or string them along while they are making up their minds, and this behavior is unfair to the person they are dating. The ENFP needs to be honest with potential partners about their need to move slowly when entering serious relationships. They cannot allow their need to please others to cloud their moral judgment.

Idealizing Potential Partners

As a rule, ENFPs almost always see the best in people. Introverted feeling is quick to pick out what it loves about someone and then extroverted intuition has a tendency to run wild making generalizations about him or her. If the person likes one song the ENFP likes, they decide that this person has the world's best taste in music. If they anticipate the ENFP's needs once, they are psychics. If they show emotional vulnerability in one instance, they are deep and compassionate healers who will take away all of the ENFP's pain before they even feel it. While it's lovely to perceive and imagine the best in others, the ENFP has to be careful not to let their fantasies get away from them. They may find themselves disappointed by their partner's reality if they are regularly indulging in fantasies about him or her. They may even take this out on their partner, covertly blaming them for not living up to the expectations that the ENFP has mentally cultivated for them.

How to work around it:

The ENFP needs to be conscious of their tendency to idealize partners in order to approach the relationship healthily. When they feel let down by their partner, the ENFP ought to take a moment to reflect on the standard they were holding their partner to. Is one that their partner actually committed to living up to, or is it one that the ENFP was projecting onto them? Being aware of their own tendency to idealize others will help the ENFP to apply more reasonable judgment to conflicts as they arise.

Smothering partners

ENFPs are all-or-nothing people and they see relationships as no exception. Though they may show initial indifference or indecision when entering a relationship, once the ENFP fully commits to it, he or she will throw as much energy as possible into making the relationship thrive. The constant flow of attention, admiration and validation that the ENFP both gives out and expects to receive from partners may be overwhelming to the other party. They may be confused by the ENFP's hot-and-cold nature and find their sudden hyper-focus on the relationship smothering.

How to avoid it:
ENFPs tend to smother partners as a means of affirming that their partner feels as strongly for the ENFP as the ENFP does for them. To lessen this need for constant validation, the ENFP should talk to their partner about how he or she shows love – perhaps it is through showing affection or doing small favors. If the ENFP is able to perceive their partner showing love in a way that comes naturally to him or her, their need for validation will be fulfilled in a subtler manner.

The ENFP may also benefit from letting their partner know

how they prefer to receive love. If physical touch is important to them, they may let their partner know that a hug means a lot to them at the end of a long day. If they particularly relish compliments, they may let their partner know that positive affirmation is important to them. As with any relationship, open communication is the best method of resolving interpersonal differences and developing strategies that both parties feel comfortable with.

Perceiving greener grass elsewhere

ENFPs see possibility everywhere and when it comes to relationships, the grass always seems greener in the relationships they aren't in. This whimsical type prefers fantasy to reality – which means that if they're feeling restless inside of a relationship, they'll turn to fantasizing about alternate relationships they could be having instead. They may assume that whatever they're lacking in their partner they could find in a different relationship with someone else. The 'one foot out the door' phenomenon is common for ENFPs in relationships, particularly when the honeymoon phase wanes and their partner's realities begin sinking in.

How to work around it:
The first step toward overcoming the grass-is-greener syndrome is for the ENFP to recognize that for them, it is entirely normal. Ne-dominant types see possibilities everywhere and can often become overwhelmed trying to balance and pursue each one. The ENFP needs to realize

that just because their extroverted intuition is running amok and their introverted feeling is supporting it, their extroverted thinking does not have to act on their feelings.

ENFPs are notoriously bad at letting their feelings pass. Because their primary decision-making function is a feeling function, they are usually quick to assume that their feelings reflect a deep truth about themselves, and they therefore must act on those feelings. However, as the ENFP develops their extroverted thinking and introverted sensing, they will become better at noticing their feelings and then releasing them, rather than acting on them. Many ENFPs have reported mindfulness or meditation practices helping them in this respect.

The more aware the ENFP becomes of his or her erratic desires, the better he or she will become at managing them. They may be able to detect a myriad of emotions when the grass-is-greener syndrome hits, such as, "I am feeling restless. I am feeling external desire. I am feeling dissatisfied within my own relationship."

At this point, the mindful ENFP can choose which emotion to focus his or her attention on. If they wish to maintain the health of their current relationship, they can turn their attention to processing and releasing their feelings of external desire. They may also take a moment to sit with the feelings of deprivation, let the weight of its negativity sink in, and then finally release it.

Once they have processed their feelings of desire, the ENFP can fully refocus their extroverted intuition on their own relationship. If they are feeling dissatisfied, they can brainstorm methods of spicing the relationship up and returning it to health. Extroverted intuition is a powerful function that can deteriorate a relationship when it turns its eye outward, but it can also go a long way toward saving a relationship if it focuses its sights on creating a happier, healthier connection between partners.

Manipulating partners

Whether they are aware of it or not, ENFPs are natural manipulators. Introverted feeling provides startlingly accurate insights into what motivates people and extroverted intuition is constantly on the hunt for shortcuts or workarounds of any kind. These natural inclinations often result in manipulative behavior on the ENFP's part, which the ENFP may not even be aware that they are engaging in!

Extroverted intuition and introverted feeling give the ENFP a natural gauge on just how far a person can be pushed, strung along or led on before they reach a breaking point. The immature ENFP may use this knowledge to their advantage – often as a means of making people believe that they are more invested in them than they really are. If the other person begins to suspect something is fishy, the ENFP's introverted feeling jumps in with a remarkably sincere display of flattery, adoration and attention, putting the other person's mind at ease.

ENFPs are both sincerely loving and indiscriminately opportunistic. They feel genuine emotion for others but are ceaselessly attracted to exploring all the options available to them. Most ENFPs view this inner conflict as a genuine tug-of-war, and fail to realize the fact that it gives way to a plethora of manipulative behaviors.

The ENFP may see their hot-and-cold behavior as a means of being true to themselves – after all, their feelings do change with high frequency and they are acting from a place of authenticity. But they fail to acknowledge that others do not understand their internal tug-of-war. Less conflicted types are likely to take the ENFP's displays of emotion at face value and believe that they are forming a long-lasting relationship with the ENFP, when the ENFP may not share that intention.

Unhealthy ENFPs may fully recognize their manipulative abilities and use them to their advantage. They will play on the desires and weaknesses of others in subtle ways, getting them to behave in a way that is beneficial for the ENFP. The reason the ENFP is capable of being such a powerful manipulator is because unlike the smooth-talking ExTP types who are also prone to manipulative tendencies, the ENFP is able to access a deep well of genuine emotion that helps them plea their case. They are able to come across as incredibly sincere, and in many cases even believe themselves to be sincere when they are, in fact, behaving in a highly manipulative manner.

How to work around it:

The first step the ENFP must take to overcome their manipulative tendencies is to acknowledge them. The ENFP always wants to think of him or herself as a highly principled individual, so coming to terms with their manipulative tendencies may be difficult for them. It may help them to recognize that their manipulations were not always intentional and that they are now taking steps to become a better friend or partner.

The ENFP must then practice honest, direct communication. It may help them to pause before responding to important questions and ask themselves, "Does what I'm about to say reflect how I'm truly feeling or does it only reflect the perception I want the other person to have?" As much as possible, the ENFP must strive to reflect their feelings and thoughts to others not just as they exist in the moment, but as they exist on a greater scale.

For example, an ENFP who is entering into a relationship may tell their partner, "I'm crazy about you and I can't get enough of you." To their partner, this may convey a sense of security. However, the ENFP may also feel unsure about whether or not they'd like a relationship to develop. By letting their partner know, "I'm crazy about you but I'm also only looking for a casual relationship right now," They are practicing honest, direct communication that allows their partner to make an informed decision about the relationship. It is important for the ENFP to remember that withholding information from others can be every bit as manipulative as outright lying.

The inability to leave bad relationships

Despite their initial reluctance to enter serious relationships, ENFPs usually experience a difficult time leaving them once they've gone bad. Just as they are slaves to perceiving greener pastures elsewhere, ENFPs also see those greener pastures within their relationships.

When things take a turn for the worse, the ENFP's introverted sensing feeds memories of happier times into their extroverted intuition, and extroverted intuition remains optimistic about their ability to re-create those positive feelings and experiences in the future. The ENFP sees fixing the relationship as a challenge that they can rise to if they simply try hard enough. This determined type hates admitting defeat and they may fight for a relationship long after it becomes obvious – even to them – that they are fighting a losing battle.

How to work around it:

Rather than clinging mercilessly to memories of happier times, the ENFP needs to engage their judging functions (that is, introverted feeling and extroverted thinking) to evaluate the current state of the relationship. They need to recognize that their wellbeing is just as important – if not more important – than their need to rise to every challenge they come across.

The more they attempt to fix an unhealthy relationship, the greater a toll the process will take on them. In some cases, the ENFP will need to exhaust every available option for making the relationship work before their extroverted intuition grows tired and finally allows introverted feeling and extroverted thinking to evaluate the true state of affairs and call the relationship quits.

ENFP Answers: Should I Leave My Partner To Pursue A Stronger Attraction?

Earlier this year, while running an MBTI-based advice series, I received the following ask from an anonymous ENFP. They expressed one of the most common ENFP relationship dilemmas – determining whether they should stay with their current partner or leave the relationship to pursue greener pastures elsewhere. The anonymous asker hit on an issue ENFP has gotten stuck on at some point – how do you decide between two hypothetical futures, when you don't know which one would bring you the most happiness?

Anonymous Asks:

> I am an ENFP. I have been in a relationship for 4 years with someone that I love. He is wonderful and we have the same values in life and in what we want to do in the future. Last year I met someone that I was very attracted to. I know that it was lust, and really I barely know this other person, but I have been thinking about them constantly and I don't know what to do. I don't understand why I can never be satisfied in a relationship! Part of me wants to end my relationship to pursue this other person… or any other person, just to feel that excitement and passion that could be stronger with someone else. I don't understand and hate myself for feeling this way, because I just feel like I will

never be satisfied and so I can never be happy. What do I do? Is there any way you can help me understand myself and how I can be satisfied?

ENFP Answers:

I once heard that we ask for advice when we already know the answer but wish that we did not. For this reason, I try to look for clues in the questions people ask to determine which response their heart needs most. With your question, Anonymous, I'm unsure. Your heart seems genuinely torn and so here is what I am going to do: I'm going to give you both the answers you've asked for and I'm going to leave it to you to decide which one feels right.

The first answer doesn't relate directly to your situation but it does relate to being an ENFP. Because here's the thing: we are indecisive folk. We see possibilities everywhere. We get so caught up in the what-could-be that we forget what is and I know that more than anyone. It's intoxicating and it's infuriating. We want it all.

When I was nineteen years old I was madly in love. It's easy to be madly in love when you're nineteen because your hormones are going crazy and you're having the best sex of your life and everything feels surreal. But I also wanted to go see the world. I wanted to get out and have all those crazy experiences you can only have when you're young and single and free. I wanted foreign boys and passionate on-the-road romances. I deliberated over staying-or-going for almost a full year. I drove everyone I knew crazy. My ESFJ mother was exhausted by my stress and indecisiveness. At the end of a particularly agonizing phone conversation, she sighed and told me, "I hope that someday you find peace."

Long after I hung up the phone, that phrase stayed with me. 'Peace' was not a feeling I had ever striven for – to the point where it shocked me that she suggested it as an option. I wondered what peace meant. I wondered what it felt like. I became moderately stressed over the idea that I might never find it. I told all this to my INFJ best friend.

Being who she was, my friend wrote a song. The only lyric I remember is, 'Some hope that you will find peace – I only hope you get a window seat.' And I immediately wished that I could get those song lyrics tattooed on my heart.

Here is what my best friend knew when she wrote that song that both myself and my mother did not – I was not on the hunt for peace at that time in my life. Later in life I would be and I would find my own route there, but for the time being I was allowed to not want peace. I was allowed to want chaos and madness and romance and window seats. I'd become so accustomed to listening to the advice of people who were vastly unlike me that I'd forgotten all of that – that peace didn't have to be the end goal. Not yet and maybe not ever.

And that is the first option that I want to give you, dear Anonymous. The option of not finding peace, if you don't want it. The option of being restless. The option of breaking out of the relationship you're in and grabbing everything you want out of life with both fists, until you've exhausted yourself to the core. I want you to know that you're allowed to leave –

for no other reason than you want to. Than you want someone else. Than you want those butterflies, that passion, that whirlwind feeling that you're worried you'll never feel again. Life doesn't have to be a search for peace and tranquility. It's allowed to be madness. It's allowed to be passion. It's allowed to be all about you and the life that you want. You're allowed to choose your window seat, Anonymous, the way I chose mine. And it may even be what helps you find peace in the long run.

Here's your second option. You have a boyfriend who loves you and whom you love back. You share the same values. You want the same things. Those are rare gems to find in a person whom you also love romantically and it seems like you already know that.

And yet, you are attracted to someone else. There is someone else whose clothing you want to rip off, whose lips you want to kiss, whose body you want all over yours. They have a word for this phenomenon and it is 'normal.' It's not even an ENFP thing: Everyone in the history of the Universe who has been in a serious relationship for a significant period of time has wanted to be with someone else. Some people ignore this impulse. Others give into it. Others walk just far enough toward the abyss to realize that they don't want to fall in. Of those three options, if you want to stay happy and healthy in love, I can only advise the first (and okay, maybe the third).

Because here's the thing: You are never going to not want other people – this is both an ENFP phenomenon and a basic human one. Our brains are specifically wired to see opportunity everywhere and lust after what we don't have. It doesn't matter how perfect your partner is or how perfect of a partner you are – somewhere down the line you are going to have a crazy, out-of-your-mind attraction to someone else and you are going to want to pursue it. I've never been in a relationship where I haven't felt that way at some point and I'm guessing neither has anyone else.

Here's the unfortunate thing about personality: You don't get to choose the way you're wired. You don't get to stop being a person who sees every opportunity and wants every option under the sun. But you do get to decide how you manage your own brain. Do you pursue all of those options with fervor or do you refocus your energy on your own relationship? Do you chase the unknown or do you develop what you already have at home? I'm not suggesting that either of these options is the superior one – I've tried them both and found each of them to be satisfying in their own right. Only you can decide which one you need right now.

Here is what I *can* tell you about your personality (and perhaps this is the answer you've been looking for all along): Your cognitive functions develop in descending order. Your extroverted thinking is immensely helpful when it comes to staying faithful – it listens to what your introverted feeling wants and then makes a concrete plan to achieve it. The thing is, as ENFPs, we can sometimes get so obsessed with dwelling in our extroverted intuition (that is, examining all the possibilities out there) that we forget to pay our introverted feeling adequate attention and therefore are shit at making decisions based on how we feel. We are afraid of what we'll find if we sit with our feelings and so we ignore them. And that is exactly what you must not do in a situation such as this.

Because there is no miracle answer to this question (aside

from pursuing polyamory). There is no have-it-all solution that your extroverted intuition is going to magically come up with. I know that's what you want, Anonymous (and don't we all) but in this case, it doesn't exist. In this case, there is only you and your heart.

Right now, you need to think through how you feel about both options. Consider that you may never feel that crazy, passionate, over-the-moon feeling of meeting someone new ever again. Then, entertain the notion that you're never going to feel the intimacy, comfort and support that you feel with your particular partner ever again. Sit right inside the feelings – process them, acknowledge them, cry over them a little if you need to. But don't run away from them. Don't rescue them with possibilities and but-maybes. Let them nestle fully inside your heart and stay there. And then ask your heart which situation feels more wrong. Which feeling you cannot live without. Because that is the answer you need.

Here is the good news in all of this, dearest Anonymous – you're an inspirer. You're a champion. You are going to be over-the-moon fantastic at whichever option you put your mind to – because that's how your brain is wired. You'll find wonderful possibilities with other people if you leave or you'll find wonderful possibilities within your relationship if you stay. For ENFPs, the decision itself is the hard part. Once you've made it, your extroverted intuition will jump back into play and make sure that you're making the absolute most out of whatever option you've chosen.

So let your heart make this decision, Anonymous. Because you're going to be happy either way.

Best of luck,
ENFP

ENFPs and Breakups

When an ENFP finally exits a relationship, their corresponding behavior will depend on the nature of the relationship and how it ended.

If the relationship was brief or if the ENFP did not feel particularly emotionally invested, they will likely have little trouble switching their focus back to the future and pursuing new opportunities.

If, however, the ENFP lacks closure or was heavily emotionally invested in the relationship, they may have an incredibly difficult time moving on. Unhealthy ENFPs may revert to relying on their introverted sensing after a breakup and become obsessed with the mistakes they made during the relationship, or become fixated on winning their ex-partner back.

Regardless of how the relationship ended, there are several things every ENFP must keep in mind when they are going through a breakup.

1. Understand that what's lost is lost. ENFPs are tireless optimists. They see the opportunity within everything and that attitude too often extends to breakup.

If the ENFP has been dumped, they may fall victim to the

'What-If's: A dire situation in which they allow introverted sensing to comb through every mistake they made throughout the course of the relationship and wonder what would have happened if they'd behaved differently. The ENFP may become convinced that they can win their ex back by owning up to past mistakes and rectifying what they've done wrong.

If the ENFP was the dumper or if the breakup was mutual, they may experience the 'What-If's in the form of second-guessing their decision. Their extroverted intuition may berate them with ways they could have made the relationship work and deem them a failure for having called it quits. In this state, the ENFP may be tempted to contact their ex and reverse the breakup.

In order to move on from a breakup, the ENFP must find a way to avoid dwelling in the 'What-If's. They must draw on input from their introverted feeling and extroverted thinking to remind themselves that the relationship ended for a reason – one or both parties were not happy, and no amount of combing through past mistakes can fix that. The ENFP must accept the breakup as absolute and unchangeable before they are able to take the first steps toward moving on.

2. Don't deny yourself the pain. More than a few ENFPs have fallen victim to a dominant-tertiary loop in the wake of a painful breakup. Rather than processing their feelings about the relationship ending, the ENFP may distract themselves by planning new adventures, accomplishing new goals and completely avoiding any semblance of alone time. While all of these activities are healthy in moderation, the ENFP needs to be careful not to neglect their emotional needs altogether. Taking the time to grieve the end of a relationship is a healthy component of moving on – and denying oneself the opportunity to do so will only cause the pain to manifest unhealthily in the long run.

3. Engage your introverted sensing in a healthy manner. As with any painful event, breakups have the potential to trigger a downward spiral in which introverted sensing manifests negatively as the ENFP's temporary dominant function. The best way for the ENFP to avoid this is to engage their introverted sensing in a healthy and positive manner following a breakup. They may make a point of exercising regularly, sustaining a healthy diet and maintaining order in their external environment as best as possible.

Long-term relationships often provide the ENFP with a source of external structure that is psychologically comforting for them. The end of a relationship therefore causes an upset to their introverted sensing – the routines and rituals they shared with their significant other no longer act as a source of stability for them. To counter-act this upset, the ENFP needs to purposefully establish a new framework of external structure. Through the deliberate implementation of productive routines, they will engage their introverted sensing in a healthy way and avoid falling victim to the negative manifestation of their inferior function.

4. Avoid idealizing past relationships. Just as some ENFPs are prone to falling into a dominant-tertiary loop after a breakup, others are prone to falling victim to their introverted feeling – they may retreat to process the breakup and end up doing a bit more processing than is necessary. The ever-optimistic ENFP may find themselves idealizing the past relationship: remembering only the good parts of what transpired and ignoring the negative aspects that actually caused them to break up. This puts them at risk of falling into the negative cycle of 'What-If's.

In order to avoid idealizing the relationship that has passed, the ENFP may need to take tangible action against their fanciful thoughts. They may force themselves to make a list of reasons why the relationship ended that they can re-read on days when they are missing their ex-partner. They may also ask their friends to dole out some tough love and remind them honestly why the relationship didn't work.

In any case, the ENFP must remember to maintain a healthy balance of alone time and people time following a difficult breakup. Regardless of how introspective they feel, the ENFP is still an extrovert and they will ultimately find it easiest to move on when they are balancing their alone time with time spent actively engaging with the world around them.

5. Be open to re-defining the future. ENFPs are incredibly future-focused. When a relationship ends, they may experience difficulty letting go of their projections for the future that included their partner. The final frontier of any breakup for an ENFP is allowing him or herself to entertain visions of the future that do not include their ex partner, and to begin moving toward that future in concrete ways.

Once they are comfortable doing this, the ENFP will find themselves well on their way to moving on.

19

ENFPs As Parents

ENFPs make for warm, enthusiastic, supportive, and loving parents. This type approaches life with a childlike energy regardless of their age and they revel in the opportunity to share that energy with children of their own.

Because ENFPs are uninhibited and fun loving by nature, they may experience difficulty balancing their role as their child's confidant and their role as a disciplinarian. ENFPs dislike disciplining their children, but feel strongly about teaching them proper morals. They can become quite strict if they discover their child has been behaving in a way that contradicts one of their own core values, and can switch almost instantly from their role as a silly, fun-loving companion to a strict, no-nonsense disciplinarian.

One of the ENFP's greatest strengths as a parent lies in their ability to understand their children on a deep level and to adapt to his or her specific needs. ENFP parents tend to put an incredible amount of effort into understanding what makes their children tick and supporting them in the specific way that they need to be supported.

The temperament of their child will, of course, have a significant influence on the relationship the ENFP forms with him or her. Though one's Myers-Briggs personality type theoretically does not solidify until one's teen years, many

ENFP parents attempt to pick up on temperamental cues from their children early on, in order to discover what their children need from them as a parent.

NF Children

- ENFPs often find they experience a particularly strong emotional connection with their intuitive, feeling children.
- The ENFP may serve as a mentor for their NF children, who are likely to share many of the ENFP's values and morals.
- ENFPs can support their NF children by taking the time to deeply understand their feelings and responding to their emotional needs.
- NF children may respond best to forms of discipline that teach them right from wrong and make them realize why their behavior was hurtful towards others.

NT Children

- ENFPs often find they experience a strong intellectual connection with their intuitive, thinking children.
- The ENFP may find that their relationship with their NT children resembles that of a teacher-student relationship.
- ENFPs can support their NT children by exploring

their intellectual interests alongside them and facilitating their quest for knowledge.

- NT children may respond best to forms of discipline that help them understand why their behavior was ineffective and why behaving in a different manner would be more beneficial in the future.

SP Children

- ENFPs often find that their relationship with their SP children revolves mainly around exploring new activities together.
- The ENFP may serve as a companion and guardian to their children as they explore various physical pursuits.
- ENFPs can support their SP children by providing them with a structured environment that encourages physical and creative exploration.
- SP children may respond best to a direct action-and-consequence style of discipline, in which they can perceive the concrete outcome of their actions.

SJ Children

- ENFPs often find their relationship with their sensing, judging children to be one that is heavily rooted in traditional family roles.
- SJ children place a high value on authority, which

means they will expect the ENFP to serve as their rule-setter and disciplinarian.

- ENFPs can support their SJ children by providing them with a high degree of structure and informing them of all the various rules they are expected to follow, both within the household and in society.
- SJ children respond best to forms of discipline that elucidate exactly what the rules are and why they need to be followed in order for things to run smoothly.

20

ENFPs And Conflict

When it comes to dealing with conflict, ENFPs tend to naturally default to one of three confrontation styles: Explosive, Accommodating, or Avoidant. All three styles are naturally engrained in the ENFP personality, but which one they naturally gravitate towards depends on how they were raised (that is, how they experienced and came to understand conflict in childhood) as well as what their Enneagram type is. All ENFPs are capable of using all three conflict styles at various points in their lives – many choose avoidant until they reach a breaking point and turn to explosive, or vice versa.

Regardless of which strategy they're naturally inclined to use, the ENFP ought to work towards achieving an Assertive confrontation style. This style allows them to express their feelings in a firm yet fair manner, without offending the other party or compromising their own desires.

Explosive

This style of conflict takes a heated, head-on approach to the issue at hand. ENFPs who have a confrontational or 'explosive' reaction to conflict are often quick to anger and may be slightly out of touch with their introverted feeling function.

They will bypass their underlying feelings of hurt or disappointment when something does not go their way, and move directly into shaming or manipulating the other party in an attempt to get what they want (exercising unhealthy extroverted thinking, rather than healthy introverted feeling).

The explosive conflict style may be particularly favored by Enneagram types 7, 8 and 3 – all of whom may see conflict as an obstacle to overcome, rather than a means of resolving an underlying issue. ENFPs who respond to conflict explosively display the following confrontation tactics:

- Quick to accuse the other party of wrongful or morally corrupt behavior.
- Unwilling to accept blame for their own wrongful actions.
- May play on the other party's insecurities and weaknesses, behaving in an uncharacteristically cruel manner.
- May have a history of feeling deeply misunderstood or unheard in conflict situations.
- Likely to experience a strong visceral reaction to anger and may feel out of control of their own reaction.
- May make rash decisions in the heat of the moment, such as breaking up with a partner or quitting a job, to prove their conviction.

The main issue at play with this style of conflict is the ENFP's tendency to jump between their extroverted intuition function (which suggests manipulative tactics) and their extroverted thinking function (which causes them to make rash decisions while angry), without fully processing their emotions via their introverted feeling. Ironically, a wounded introverted feeling is likely to be subconsciously driving the entire explosion.

In order to move from an explosive communication style to an assertive one, the ENFP needs to become more comfortable with their introverted feeling function. By taking the time to process negative emotions internally, the ENFP will be able to understand the root of their anger and pinpoint its origin. Anger is almost always masking a deeper negative emotion, which the ENFP must understand before they are able to approach the issue consciously and productively.

When the ENFP understands the true root of their anger, they can then turn to their extroverted thinking to find productive methods of resolving it. They may approach the other party in a calm manner and explain their feelings honestly. They can then present options for a resolution that serves both parties. It is impossible for the ENFP to be assertive without fully understanding the underlying feeling they are experiencing – but once they do, they can use their extroverted thinking to approach conflict assertively and productively.

Accommodating

This style of conflict is passive and compromising. When a confrontation is necessary, ENFPs who use this style tend to agree to the alternate party's way of resolving the issue, without adequately raising or arguing his or her own point of view. It is often used by ENFPs who place a high value on interpersonal harmony and seek to put conflict to bed at all costs. This style may be favored by ENFPs who have underdeveloped extroverted thinking, who suffer from low self-esteem or who place more stock into their relationship with the opposing party than their attachment to the issue at hand.

The accommodating conflict style may be particularly favored by Enneagram Types 2 and 9, both of whom feel highly uncomfortable with conflict. Indicators of an accommodating confrontation style are as follows:

- Feels deeply uncomfortable when the peace is disrupted.
- May feel hesitant to overtly raise his or her point of view during conflict.
- Avoids any sort of conflict unless it is absolutely necessary to enter into.
- Often makes subtle adjustments to his or her behavior to accommodate the other party, without being asked.
- Values the happiness of their partner above their own happiness.
- Feels incapable of providing a superior solution to that of the opposing party's (despite the fact that they may not agree with the opposing party's solution).
- Fears voicing their opinion for fear that they will hurt someone's feelings or have their own hurt.

Many ENFPs are accommodating by nature. Because this type is not particularly fussed by small, day-to-day concerns, they tend to be open and agreeable towards other peoples' ways of going about things. However, this passive confrontation style becomes a problem if and when the ENFP elects to go against his or her personal values simply to maintain the peace.

ENFPs who employ an accommodating conflict style against their will often have underdeveloped extroverted thinking (and therefore consider themselves incapable of supplying a superior solution to the problem at hand), or suffer from low self-esteem (and therefore submit to the opposing party as a means of gleaning validation that they are a good, agreeable person).

In either case, the ENFP needs to work through their introverted feeling to determine their definitive stance on the issue and then turn to their extroverted thinking to produce a solution. At this stage, the ENFP may benefit from speaking with a friend or loved one who exhibits strong extroverted thinking skills. For many ENFPs, assertive confrontation is a skill that must be practiced – but it begins with taking a firm stance on the issue at hand and having a tangible solution available that her or she can present with confidence.

Avoidant

This style of conflict is passive but uncompromising. Rather than engaging in confrontation (even when it is glaringly necessary), ENFPs with an avoidant confrontation style will altogether avoid the opposing party or drop them from their lives. The ENFP may convince themselves that they are unappreciated by the other person and are better of without them. They may approach this decision from a place of insecurity (secretly fearing that they will 'lose' the confrontation if they engage in it) or from a place of perceived superiority (deciding the person or conflict at hand is not worth their attention).

The avoidant conflict style is used by all types under certain circumstances, but may be the chosen method of conflict resolution for 4s and 7s. Whereas the 4 may not want to waste their time on anyone who doesn't understand them, the 7 may not want to confront the negative feelings involved in the conflict and instead distract themselves with positive experiences. Those who employ an avoidant confrontation style may exhibit the following behaviors:

- May feel threatened in some way by the opposing party's point of view.
- May fear that resolving the conflict at hand will force them to compromise their pride.
- May feel misunderstood by the other party to the point where they view the conflict as unresolvable.
- Likely to view their own perspective as one that they are entirely unwilling to compromise on (this may be the product of particularly active introverted feeling).

ENFPs who choose avoidance as a main method of conflict resolution tend to be particularly stubborn. They may be protecting a value judgment they've reached through their introverted feeling or they may be avoiding their introverted feeling altogether. Either way, the ENFP must learn to confront the problem in a healthy, productive manner if they don't want to lose the other person as a result.

In order to move from an avoidant confrontation strategy to an assertive one, the ENFP must pinpoint what is keeping him or her from confronting the problem. If it is a lack of self-confidence, they may refer to the strategies used to overcome an accommodating confrontation style. If it is an attempt to avoid processing their deeper feelings on the issue at hand, they may refer to the strategies used to overcome an explosive confrontation style.

In either case, the ENFP must learn to break down the feeling of pride that is berating their introverted feeling and attempt to see the situation from the opposing party's point of view. They may engage their extroverted intuition here and attempt to understand what is driving the other person's thoughts and actions. Only once they do this can the ENFP move toward understanding his or her own feelings about the situation and move towards a positive resolution.

Part 6

How To Make It Work With Every Type

21

Inter-Type Compatibility

It is important to note that *type alone does not determine compatibility, nor does it predict the success of a given relationship.* Though some types are prone to understanding each other more naturally than other types, there are a variety of factors that contribute to the success or failure of a given relationship – many of which are completely unrelated to the Myers-Briggs type indicator.

The relationship techniques and tools that are presented in the following chapter are meant to be applied to relationships in which both parties are committed to understanding one another and strengthening their connection. They are not miracle methods for making your crush like you back. They are not one-sided solutions to relationship issues. These tools require the cooperation of both parties and, like any healthy relationship, they begin with both of the individuals involved deciding that the relationship is worth putting some work into.

Many of the tips provided inference the existence of a romantic relationship between the ENFP and type in question. However, any of these tools can be applied to relationships of any nature. Use them to work things out with your mother. To smooth things over with your infuriating colleague. To patch things up with an old, neglected friend.

The aim of this chapter is to provide you with an understanding of the inter-type conflicts that may arise due to differences in cognitive functions and how to work around them in a way that is as painless as possible for everyone involved.

The Other Four Cognitive Functions

In order to understand other types and how we relate to them, we must first understand the cognitive functions that we as ENFPs do not possess.

Rather than presenting these functions in a vacuum, I chose to contrast them with the ENFP's functions, which you are already familiar with. It is important to understand what a profound difference the orientation of a given function (that is, whether it is introverted or extroverted) makes on its expression. The more we understand the differences between ourselves and other types, the more we can grow to overcome and appreciate those differences.

Introverted Intuition (Ni)

- Whereas extroverted intuition synthesizes and builds on new ideas, introverted intuition breaks down and analyzes pre-existing ideas.
- Whereas extroverted intuition indiscriminately examines multiple possibilities for the future,

introverted intuition seeks to determine the best of all possible options for the future.

- Whereas extroverted intuition is inherently creative and open-ended, introverted intuition is inherently analytical and discerning.
- Whereas extroverted intuition explores how to connect and expand on pre-existing ideas, introverted intuition examines how to relate and categorize pre-existing ideas.

Extroverted Feeling (Fe)

- Whereas introverted feeling examines emotions through the lens of what is authentic and true, extroverted feeling looks at emotions through the lens of what is useful in maintaining interpersonal harmony.
- Whereas introverted feeling believes we ought to "Live and let live," extroverted feeling believes we ought to find a way to all live in connection and harmony with one another.
- Whereas introverted feeling believes in authenticity at all costs, extroverted feeling believes in compromising individual traits or desires for the good of the group.
- Whereas introverted feeling seeks to understand emotion first and manage it second, extroverted feeling seeks to manage emotion first and understand it second.

Introverted Thinking (Ti)

- Whereas extroverted thinking looks at what is tangibly useful, introverted thinking looks at what is indisputably true.
- Whereas extroverted thinking implements plans, introverted thinking analyses systems.
- Whereas extroverted thinking is results-oriented, introverted thinking is process-oriented.
- Whereas extroverted thinking strives to impose order on chaos, introverted thinking strives to comprehensively understand the chaos within order.

Extroverted Sensing (Se)

- Whereas introverted sensing categorizes experiences, extroverted sensing collects them.
- Whereas introverted sensing references past experiences when encountering new situations, extroverted sensing references present stimuli when encountering new situations.
- Whereas introverted seeks to identify order within its environment, extroverted sensing seeks to explore the chaos of their environment.
- Whereas introverted sensing plans for the future, extroverted sensing experiences the future as it comes.

Note:

It's important to keep in mind that even types who share all four of our cognitive functions may think and act in vastly differently ways than we do, as the order of functions is just as important in determining compatibility as the functions themselves.

Think of the functions as furniture, and the order they appear in as the layout of that furniture. Some types may have all of the same furniture as you, but have it laid out so differently that their home is almost entirely unrecognizable to you. Other types may have different furniture than you do, but have it arranged in a way so similar to your own arrangement that you feel a natural comfort in their home.

22

How To Make It Work With Every Type

INTJ

Cognitive Functions: Ni – Te – Fi – Se

INTJs are the stoic, intellectual masterminds of the MBTI. ENFPs tend to be drawn to this type because of their intensity, their complexity and their grounded presence. INTJs find themselves drawn to the ENFP because of their enthusiasm, their complexity and their intellectually explorative attitude. Many MBTI theorists consider the ENFP-INTJ pairing to be among the most fitting matches within the Myers-Briggs inventory for long-term partnership.

These types share only two functions (Te and Fi), but the INTJ's dominant introverted intuition is an excellent complement to the ENFP's dominant extroverted intuition. They are both big-picture thinkers, though they approach the 'bigger picture' differently. Using Ni, the INTJ takes a holistic approach to ideas – aiming to hone in on the most accurate explanation for every situation and fit what they know into their complex internal framework. The ENFP, on the other hand, is intellectually explorative – they aim to synthesize and entertain a seemingly infinite number of novel ideas. The ENFP works as something of an idea-generator, whereas the INTJ works as something of an idea-optimizer. Together, they are an intellectual dream team.

On a day-to-day basis, the INTJ is focused, pragmatic and detail-oriented, whereas the ENFP is enthusiastic, passionate and spontaneous. The INTJ appreciates and benefits from the ENFP's social competence, whereas the ENFP appreciates and benefits from the INTJ's grounded presence and sense of responsibility. Because each type's tertiary function is the other's auxiliary, there is a certain ease of understanding that arises between these two types when both are healthy and well developed.

However, that is not to say that this pairing is without its challenges.

Potential Challenges:

- Having non-dominant introverted feeling in one's stacking leads to a sense of stubbornness – which both the ENFP and the INTJ possess in high measure.
- Because both types are introverted feelers, they tend to be somewhat emotionally guarded (the INTJ more so than the ENFP), often leading to communication difficulties.
- Both types are prone to narcissistic tendencies while unhealthy, which has the potential to manifest negatively within the relationship.
- Having an auxiliary feeling function, the ENFP tends

to require more affection, affirmation and validation than the INTJ feels comfortable giving.

- Having a dominant introverted function, the INTJ may require more alone time than the ENFP feels comfortable providing.

How to make it work:

- INTJs respond well to honest, direct communication. If a problem arises, explain it as calmly and rationally as possible to the INTJ – they genuinely do want to resolve issues that arise and will probably be keen to listen.
- Respect their need for independence within the relationship and appreciate that they respect yours.
- Display loyalty and honesty in your relationship with an INTJ – trust and commitment within a relationship is incredibly important to them.
- Recognize the ways in which they show love – they may not be the most romantic partner or emotionally expressive friend, but they display their affection through acts of loyalty, commitment and diligence.
- Be open and direct about your needs within the relationship – they are important, but not always immediately recognizable to the INTJ.

ENTJ

Cognitive Functions: Te – Ni – Se – Fi

ENTJs are the analytical and tirelessly efficient leaders of the MBTI. ENFPs tend to be drawn to this type because of their confidence, gregariousness, intelligence and put-together attitude. ENTJs tend to be drawn to the ENFP because of their openness, intelligence and drive. Though appearing to be quite different on the surface, these types are surprisingly complementary.

These types share two cognitive functions (Introverted feeling and extroverted thinking), though the ENFP's auxiliary function is inferior for the ENTJ and the ENTJ's dominant function is tertiary for the ENFP. For this reason, the ENTJ-ENFP relationship is often one where a great amount of growth takes place on behalf of both parties. The ENFP can help the ENTJ access their introverted feeling and grow emotionally, whereas the ENTJ can help the ENFP develop their extroverted thinking and implement their many ideas.

The ENTJ's auxiliary function – introverted intuition – serves as an excellent complement to the ENFP's dominant extroverted intuition. The ENFP typically provides various new ideas to the ENTJ, who then turns to their extroverted thinking and introverted intuition to determine how those ideas could be optimized and implemented most effectively.

On a day-to-day basis, the ENTJ is focused, task-oriented and efficient, whereas the ENFP is creative, thoughtful and excitable. The ENTJ benefits from the ENFP's enthusiasm and outside-the-box thinking, whereas the ENFP benefits from the ENTJ's diligence, capability and follow-through. Between two well-developed types, the ENTJ-ENFP pairing is a relationship that provides a natural balance between two well-suited types.

Potential Challenges:

- The ENTJ's inferior introverted feeling may cause them to be too emotionally closed-off for the ENFP's liking.
- The ENFP may see the ENTJ as too rigid or controlling on a day-to-day basis, whereas the ENTJ may see the ENFP as overly emotional or impulsive.
- Because the ENTJ's dominant decision-making function is extroverted thinking and the ENFP's dominant decision-making function is introverted feeling, they tend to manage money vastly differently. The ENFP tends to be looser and more impulsive with their spending than the ENTJ, who is highly invested in saving and/or investing money. This may cause friction within a partnership.
- The ENFP may require more validation and affection than the ENTJ feels comfortable providing. On the flip side, the ENTJ may require more independence than the ENFP feels comfortable providing.

How to make it work:

- Be assertive with the ENTJ. When they seem as though they're being 'bossy,' they're usually just attempting to communicate what they believe the best choice to be. If you don't agree with this choice, let them know this directly and explain your reasoning to them.
- Communicate your needs honestly and directly to the ENTJ. If, for example, you require more affection or validation than they are providing, they will appreciate being told this point-blank.
- Understand and appreciate how the ENTJ shows love – they may not be particularly emotionally expressive but they will go above and beyond to solve problems that arise either within the relationship or externally.
- If you are asking the ENTJ to work on developing their introverted feeling for the good of the relationship, accept that you may need to work on developing your extroverted thinking for the same reason.
- Display loyalty to the ENTJ in all endeavors – to them, loyalty is the ultimate act of love.

ENTP

Cognitive Functions: Ne – Ti – Fe – Si

ENTPs are the enthusiastic, rational idea-generators of the MBTI. ENFPs share the ENTP's dominant function and therefore usually feel a natural connection with this type. They are drawn to the ENTP's enthusiasm, outside-the-box thinking and inventive attitude, all of which mirrors their own. The ENTP is, in turn, drawn to the ENFP's open-mindedness, intellectually explorative attitude and general zest for life. These types share a natural surface-level understanding of one another, which is usually apparent to both parties immediately.

Sharing both extroverted intuition as a dominant function and introverted sensing as an inferior function means that ENFPs and ENTPs share the majority of the same major strengths and weaknesses. Both will relish in the other's intellectually explorative attitude and will rarely feel bored around the other. However, both also have a tendency to neglect the more routine aspects of day-to-day life, such as paying bills or doing chores.

The majority of the conflict that arises between these two types stems from the ENTP possessing introverted thinking and extroverted feeling as their auxiliary and tertiary functions, whereas the ENFP possesses introverted feeling and extroverted thinking respectively. Because neither type fundamentally understands the other's decision-making functions, they often experience difficulty in the realms of emotional connection and decision-making. The emotional connection between an ENTP and an ENFP is anything but natural – however, both types enjoy a challenge. And if they take on their relationship as a challenge, these two enthusiastic types can certainly find a way to make it work.

Potential Challenges:

- Both types are prone to manipulative tactics within a relationship when unhealthy, which neither responds well to being on the receiving end of.
- The ENTP may have trouble understanding the ENFP's deep, complex emotions. On the flip side, the ENFP may have trouble understanding the ENTP's need to understand the world via cold, hard logic.
- The ENFP may be offended by the ENTP's brutally honest nature.
- The ENTP may feel smothered by the ENFP's affectionate nature.
- The ENFP may have trouble understanding the ENTP's regular method of showing love, which is more geared more toward solving their partner's problems than displaying affection overtly.

How to make it work:

- Be incredibly direct with the ENTP when a problem arises within the relationship. This type responds best to honest, straightforward communication and does not appreciate having things sugarcoated.
- Recognize that love means different things to the two of you. The ENTP experiences and displays love by helping their partner solve problems and supporting them in their endeavors. They are never going to be in touch with their feelings in the same

way as you are. This is because they have extroverted feeling – which is oriented outward, into the world of action – rather than inwards, into the world of emotional exploration.

- Be firm when it comes to personal boundaries. Unhealthy ENTPs are notorious boundary-pushers, and they need a partner who can take a firm stance against their invasive tactics.
- Be direct about what you'd like to see happen within your relationship. The ENTP takes well to a challenge, so if you tell them, "I want to work on our emotional connection," They will take better to this suggestion than they will to complaints about a lack of emotional connection.

INTP

Cognitive Functions: Ti – Ne – Si – Fe

INTPs are the rational, explorative logicians of the MBTI. ENFPs tend to be drawn to this type because of their aloof, detached nature, which presents itself as a challenge to the ENFP. The INTP is in turn drawn to the ENFP because of their curiosity and open-mindedness. Both types are laid-back on the surface but intellectually intense, which is a commonality they appreciate in one another.

These types share two cognitive functions – extroverted

intuition and introverted sensing, in a somewhat complimentary fashion. The INTP has the ENFP's dominant function as their auxiliary. Therefor, the two will be able to connect through sharing ideas, exploring theories and discussing the 'bigger picture' of the world around them. The INTP's tertiary function – introverted sensing – is the ENFP's inferior function, meaning these two may enjoy similar lifestyles but are unlikely to connect predominantly through their introverted sensing.

The INTP leads with dominant introverted thinking, which is a function that the ENFP neither possesses nor particularly understands, but may learn to appreciate in relation to the INTP's extroverted intuition. Conversely, the ENFP's auxiliary introverted feeling is difficult for the INTP to understand, but may be of interest to them. Because their feeling functions are oriented in opposite directions (introverted for the ENFP, extroverted for the INTP) and appear in vastly different places in their function stacking (auxiliary for the ENFP, inferior for the INTP), these two types may experience difficulty connecting on an emotional level.

Potential Challenges:

- The INTP may have trouble understanding the ENFP's deep, complex emotions whereas the ENFP may have trouble understanding the INTP's need to understand everything – including emotion – from a purely objective standpoint.
- The ENFP may feel emotionally neglected by the

INTP, or have their feelings hurt by their blunt, objective nature.

- The INTP may feel smothered by the affectionate ENFP, or become annoyed by their subjective method of looking at things.
- The ENFP may grow bored by the INTP's reluctance to engage with the outer world, whereas the INTP may grow exhausted by the ENFP's extroversion.
- Both parties have a tendency to be somewhat dismissive of relationships, which may kill this pairing before it has time to properly develop.

How to make it work:

- Approach conflicts by explaining your point of view as clearly and objectively as possible. Explain the facts of the situation that led you to feel a certain way.
  Recognize their willingness to work on the relationship and help you with your problems as their way of showing love.
- Be patient with the INTP's refusal to express emotion off the bat. Be open to hearing about how he or she feels, but not overly pushy or invasive. They need to feel safe and comfortable with you before opening up.

- Don't make assumptions about how the INTP is feeling. Their introverted thinking operates vastly differently than your introverted feeling, even though their process of withdrawing to think things over may look similar to yours from the outside.
- Engage the INTP's curiosity as a means of bonding with them – your shared extroverted intuition can serve as a fantastic means of bringing you closer together.

ESFP

Cognitive Functions: Se – Fi – Te – Ni

ESFPs are the lively, people-focused entertainers of the MBTI. ENFPs find themselves drawn to this type because of their adventurous, enthusiastic attitude and their shared love of people. ESFPs find themselves drawn to ENFPs predominantly for the same reasons. These types usually share a plethora of interests, passions and hobbies, as their people-loving nature attracts them to many of the same endeavors. These types make ideal partners-in-crime for one another, as they are both adventurous in spirit and tend to share a similar system of values.

These types share two cognitive functions in common – introverted feeling and extroverted thinking. Because they are stacked in the same way (Introverted feeling is auxiliary and extroverted thinking is tertiary to both parties), they approach decision-making using similar methods. This allows each party to have a natural respect for the other, as both tend to view the other's choices as similar to what they would have done in the same situation.

Of course, these types do differ on their dominant and inferior functions. The ESFP leads with Se and has inferior Ni – neither of which the ENFP possesses. Interestingly, this seems to strengthen the ENFP-ESFP relationship. The ENFP is most confident in their intuitive function and least concerned with their sensing function, whereas the ESFP is most confident in their sensing function but least concerned with their intuitive function. This means that each party's strength is the other's weakness, which allows both types to feel unthreatened by the other. There is usually a natural sense of affection that develops between ENFPs and ESFPs, though they may not take one another particularly seriously.

Potential Challenges:

- Both parties tend to be non-confrontational to the point where they'll allow issues to fester and grow rather than acknowledging them outright.
- The ENFP may feel that they are lacking a deep intellectual connection with the ESFP, who is not particularly in tune with their intuitive side.
- The ESFP may grow exasperated by the ENFP's

overly theoretical nature and their preference for analysis over action.

- Having two auxiliary introverted feelers in one relationship may lead to feelings of competition and/or become too emotionally intense for one or both partners to bear.
- Though this relationship is usually one of mutual attraction and respect, these partners do not naturally balance one another out and may therefore experience trouble maintaining a long-term romantic relationship with each other.

How to make it work:

- Stay in touch with what your ESFP is feeling and thinking – it is easy to assume that you are always on the same page because you behave so similarly, but this is not always the case.
- Find outlets for your extroverted intuition that do not involve pestering your ESFP with an endless onslaught of new theories – they may enjoy these to a point, but it is best to find other intuitive friends to explore ideas with, as they will eventually exhaust the ESFP.
- Display your affection physically – ESFPs are highly sensory-oriented and physical touch is important to them.
- Validate the ESFP – they feed off compliments and will gladly return them in kind.
- Approach criticism or conflict in a kind, caring way.

The ESFP needs to know that you still love, appreciate and respect them when you are angry or upset. They value keeping the peace and need to feel safe and comfortable around you before they are comfortable opening up about how they are truly feeling.

ISFP

Cognitive Functions: Fi – Se – Ni – Te

ISFPs are the soulful, compassionate artists of the MBTI world. The ENFP tends to be drawn to this type due to their compassion, insight and unexpectedly adventurous spirit. The ISFP, in turn, is drawn to the ENFP because of their passion, depth and enthusiasm for life. They may enjoy many of the same passions or endeavors, as they are both deeply creative individuals who appreciate the world around them on more than just a surface level.

ENFPs and ISFPs share two of the same cognitive functions – introverted feeling and extroverted thinking. Introverted feeling is dominant for the ISFP and auxiliary for the ENFP, making it the function they connect on most naturally. They will likely enjoy exploring one another's worldviews and will see eye-to-eye on many matters of morality and decision-making. Both parties also have extroverted thinking in their stacking, though it is tertiary for the ENFP and inferior for the ISFP. The ISFP will be either appreciative of or intimidated by the ENFP's assertiveness, depending on where each party is in their development. Regardless, extroverted thinking is unlikely to be a function that connects these two, as neither particularly enjoys using it unless necessary.

These types differ in in their perceptive functions. While the ENFP is a dominant extroverted intuitive, the ISFP's main perceiving function is their auxiliary function, extroverted sensing. The ENFP does not share this function but may appreciate it in the ISFP, as it is filtered through the lens of their Fi and is usually used to support their creative pursuits or show practical care and affection for their loved ones. On the flip side, the ENFP's extroverted intuition may be appreciated by the ISFP as it sources new adventurous ideas that may peak the ISFP's interest. Last but not least, the ISFP may call their tertiary introverted intuition into play while interacting with the ENFP, which can lead to intense philosophical conversations that captivate both parties.

Potential Challenges:

- The ISFP may find themselves intimidated by the ENFP's brash or straightforward nature.
- The ENFP may grow exasperated by the ISFP's initial reluctance to open up.
- The ENFP may assume they know what the ISFP is feeling but be wrong in their suspicions.
- The ENFP may feel as though they're lacking the intellectual connection they glean from fellow intuitive types.

- The ENFP may assume that because the ISFP is not saying anything, there is no problem, whereas in actuality, the ISFP often needs encouragement from their partner to voice their true thoughts and feelings. Failure to check in with the ISFP may lead to problems festering and growing.

How to make it work:

- Be patient with the ISFP – they need to feel safe and comfortable before they can open up completely. They will likely reveal pieces of themselves a little at a time – testing how you react to their revelations to determine whether or not they feel comfortable opening up further.
- Check in with your ISFP regularly in a kind, compassionate manner, to ensure that they are not feeling upset by or uncomfortable with any aspect of your relationship.
- Approach conflict kindly and patiently. Encourage your ISFP to share their point of view and do not shut down their arguments without listening to them. ISFPs need to feel safe to share their true feelings, which they will not do if you counter them with hard logic or criticism.
- If you are unhappy with some aspect of the relationship, explain your feelings to the ISFP. They truly do want their partners to be happy and will be willing to work on almost any aspect of the

relationship if the way you are feeling is brought to their awareness in a non-confrontational manner.

ESFJ

Cognitive Functions: Fe – Si – Ne – Ti

ESFJs are the friendly, practical nurturers of the MBTI world. The ENFP is drawn to this type because of their warmth, their grounded nature and their shared love of people. The ESFJ is drawn to the ENFP because of their passion, their outgoing nature and their fun-loving attitude. These two may run in similar social circles and bond over their love of bringing people together.

These two types share two cognitive functions – extroverted intuition and introverted sensing. However, what is auxiliary in the ESFJ (introverted sensing) is inferior in the ENFP and what is dominant in the ENFP (extroverted intuition) is tertiary for the ESFJ. This gives them very little common ground from a functional perspective and may interfere with them developing a long-lasting relationship.

The ESFJ leads with extroverted feeling, which the ENFP completely lacks, and the ENFP backs their extroverted intuition up with introverted feeling, which the ESFJ completely lacks. Their mismatched functions may cause friction within the relationship. However, both types take the health of their personal relationships incredibly seriously, which means that if they're both committed to making it work, the ENFP and ESFJ can certainly make their relationship thrive.

Potential Challenges:

- Because extroverted feeling and introverted feeling operate under entirely different premises, the ESFJ may see the ENFP as selfish and unaccommodating, whereas the ENFP may see the ESFJ as petty and lacking a backbone.
- The ESFJ may give tirelessly to the ENFP, who may entirely fail to notice many of the ways in which the ESFJ is accommodating them. The ESFJ may in turn feel unappreciated by the ENFP.
- The ENFP may feel misunderstood by the ESFJ and miss the intellectual connection they share with other intuitive types.
- The ESFJ may grow frustrated or stressed out by the ENFP's unpredictable behavior.
- The ENFP may feel as though the ESFJ is trying to limit or control their behavior.

How to make it work:

- When a conflict develops, reassure the ESFJ that you still love and care for them before delving into the issue.
- Recognize and respect the ESFJ's need for harmony. While you may see debates and intense

conversations as a method of intellectual connection, the ESFJ sees these as a disruption of harmony and may feel hurt by them.

- Let the ESFJ know – on a regular basis – that you notice the little things they do for you and that you love and appreciate them immensely.
- Make a point to be reliable, punctual and trustworthy with your ESFJ – this is huge to them.
- Find common interests that you can connect on. Many ENFPs find the greatest struggle within their ENFP-ESFJ relationship to be a lack of intellectual connection. However, when discussing issues or ideas that both parties feel strongly about, the ENFP and ESFJ can experience a strong intellectual connection.

ISFJ

Cognitive Functions: Si – Fe – Ti – Ne

ISFJs are the caring, responsible nurturers of the MBTI. ENFPs tend to find themselves drawn to this type because of their grounded presence, their approachable nature and their generous, giving spirit. The ISFJ finds themselves drawn to the ENFP because they admire their enthusiasm and determination as well as their passion and love for others.

These types share two cognitive functions – extroverted

intuition and introverted sensing. However, what is dominant for one type is inferior for the other, which means that their shared functions manifest vastly differently. The ISFJ leads with introverted sensing and has inferior extroverted intuition, whereas the ENFP has the opposite. If both parties are mature and well-developed, they can learn a great deal from one another – the ISFJ can help the ENFP apply structure and follow-through to his or her ideas, and the ENFP can help the ISFJ expand his or her horizons and approach problems in new ways.

These types differ on their decision-making functions. Whereas the ISFJ uses auxiliary extroverted feeling and tertiary introverted thinking to make decisions, the ENFP uses auxiliary introverted feeling and tertiary extroverted thinking. Though extroverted and introverted feeling manifest vastly differently, the ENFP and ISFJ may be surprised to find that their decision making processes are not so far off from one another. They both look at decisions through the lens of their perceptive function, and then come to a decision based on how they feel about this perception. However, the ISFJ usually bases their decision on the good of the group, whereas the ENFP basis the decision on their internal set of morals. This may eventually cause friction within the relationship, as the ISFJ may over-accommodate for the ENFP (who may not even notice them doing so).

Potential Challenges:

- ISFJs tend to communicate their needs and desires subtly – which often goes unnoticed by the ENFP.

This may lead to the ISFJ feeling neglected or unappreciated by the ENFP.

- The ENFP craves stimulation and variety, whereas the ISFJ values consistency – these lifestyle differences may cause friction within the relationship.
- The ISFJ may accommodate the ENFP's by compromising their own, which the ENFP may not even notice him or her doing.
- The ENFP may find themselves catering to the ISFJ's emotional needs but neglecting their practical ones – to an ISFJ, partnership in particular is about sharing responsibilities and duties, which does not come naturally to the ENFP.
- Conversely, the ENFP may find themselves accommodating the ISFJ too much, neglecting their own need for maintaining an active social circle outside of the relationship.

How to make it work:

- Check in regularly with the ISFJ to ensure their needs are being met. Ask what you can help them with today, or what the two of you can tackle as a team. Show enthusiasm so they do not feel guilty about enlisting your help.
- If sharing a living space, structure chores or errands so that the responsibility does not quietly fall on the ISFJ (I.e. make a cleaning schedule and stick to it).

- If the ISFJ expresses a need once, assume that it does not change unless they explicitly tell you otherwise.
- Explain to the ISFJ that having a wide social circle outside of the relationship is important to you, but that you still love and care for them. This may take some getting used to on their part.
- Show the ISFJ that you are committed to the relationship and that they can trust and rely on you. This is huge to the ISFJ. They take relationships incredibly seriously and are best paired with partners who do the same.

ISTJ

Cognitive Functions: Si – Te – Fi – Ne

ISTJs are the practical, diligent duty-fulfillers of the MBTI. They are the four letter opposite of the ENFP. However, ENFPs tend to be drawn to this type because of their natural differences – that is, the ISTJ's pragmatism, loyalty and decisiveness. The ISTJ, in turn, is attracted to the ENFP's quick wit, bubbly personality and emotional intelligence.

Despite being four letter opposites, these types share all four cognitive functions. However, they use these functions in completely opposite order and they manifest almost entirely differently. Each type leads with the other's inferior function and has their auxiliary as the other party's tertiary. This has the potential to lead to a great deal of conflict between these types if one or both parties have not developed their tertiary and inferior functions. Between two mature types, however, this relationship has the potential to be one of great growth and development.

If both partners are open to growing within the relationship, the ENFP can bring out the adventurous side of the ISTJ and help them to open up emotionally. On the flip side, the ISTJ can ground the ENFP and help them to develop follow-through for their many ideas. These types experience the world incredibly differently but can certainly learn to appreciate and grow from these differences.

Potential Challenges:

- Both types are incredibly stubborn when it comes to their personal morals and may experience extreme conflict if these values do not line up.
- The ISTJ may grow frustrated by the ENFP's behavioral inconsistencies and their tendency to 'leap before looking.'
- The ENFP may grow frustrated by how long it takes the ISTJ to warm up to new ideas and/or their reluctance to discuss alternate ways of doing things.
- The ENFP usually requires significantly more validation that the ISTJ tends to provide. They may also take the ISTJ's attempts at giving them constructive criticism as an attack on their character.
- The ISTJ may grow frustrated by the ENFP's refusal to alter their impractical behavior, despite the ISTJ

providing them with solutions. The ENFP's refusal to take the ISTJ's advice may also lead the ISTJ to feel useless within the relationship.

- Both types may feel as though the other is simply refusing to look at things from their point of view, and may consequently feel misunderstood or unheard by the other.

How to make it work:

- Find a shared interest that you can connect on – preferably one that the ISTJ can learn about in depth and that the ENFP can feel regularly challenged by. This will give you the opportunity to learn and grow as a team, in a way that highlights both parties' natural strengths.

- Discuss your needs and values overtly, to avoid misunderstandings. The ENFP may not realize, for example, that the ISTJ feels personally offended when the ENFP is not punctual. On the flip side, the ISTJ may not realize that the ENFP feels personally offended if they are not told, "I love you," on a regular basis.

- Be direct about what you need from the ISTJ. They tend to jump immediately into problem-solving mode, so if that is not what you need, tell them so overtly. The simple phrase, "I just need to rant about something," or "I've had a bad day and need a hug," will likely work wonders.

- When a conflict arises, be deliberate about

examining one another's points of view. Try having one party explain the other's point of view aloud using non-accusatory language, to ensure they understand where the other is coming from. Then, have the other party do the same.

- Work on recognizing the intention behind one another's actions. Ask yourself why the ISTJ is doing X or Y that is upsetting you – i.e. If they are offering you constructive criticism, it is probably because they love you and want to see you thrive. This can quickly diffuse feelings of hostility and allow each partner to glean a greater appreciation for the other.

ISTP

Cognitive Functions: Ti – Se – Ni – Fe

ISTPs are the systematic, hands-on logicians of the MBTI. ENFPs find themselves drawn to this type because of their nonthreatening, laid-back nature, their sense of humor and their capable personality. In turn, the ISTPs find themselves drawn to ENFPs because of their optimism, their charm and their relaxed sense of humor. Though these types have zero cognitive functions in common, they often enjoy a surprisingly natural surface-level connection.

The very reason why ENFPs and ISTPs should not get along is often the exact reason why they do – they look at everything entirely differently, but neither one is particularly set in their specific way of seeing things. They pose very little threat to one another, as each one possesses a completely unique set of strengths from the other. These types often find they get along easily and comfortably as friends or colleagues. They may experience more difficultly connecting on a romantic level, however, as these types approach love and intimacy in vastly different ways.

While the possession of an entirely different set of cognitive functions can be a challenge, it can also allow each partner to learn a great deal from the other, and provide balance within a relationship. The ENFP dwells primarily in the realm of analyzing the abstract, whereas the ISTP dwells in the realm of analyzing the concrete. The ISTP may be pleased by the ENFP's creative insight and the ENFP may appreciate the ISTP's hands-on approach to problem solving. These types may find that in many ways, they unexpectedly fill in each other's blind spots.

Potential Challenges:

- The ISTP may require more alone time than the ENFP is comfortable providing them with. On the flip side, the ISTP may feel smothered by the ENFP's emotional attentiveness.
- The ENFP may require more validation than the ISTP is comfortable giving.
- The ISTP may require more down time than the ENFP, who may feel restless as a result.
- The ISTP may struggle to understand the ENFP's

moods and ideas when they are not grounded in the concrete (i.e. If there is not a tangible reason why the ENFP is feeling a certain way, the ISTP may struggle to understand the cause of that feeling).

How to make it work:

- Respect the ISTP's need for independence and alone time within the relationship.
- Be overt about your needs within the relationship – the ISTP is unlikely to infer what you need from your abstractions, but responds well to being asked directly.
- Appreciate the ways in which the ISTP shows love – usually through loyalty, physical affection and protection, rather than verbal affirmation.
- When conflict arises, explain your reasoning to the ISTP calmly and clearly – their introverted thinking needs to understand the issue from all angles before their extroverted feeling can change its mind.

ESTJ

Cognitive Functions: Te – Si – Ne – Fi

ESTJs are the industrious, take-charge realists of the MTBI.

ENFPs find themselves drawn to this type because of their confidence, independence and drive. ESTJs find themselves drawn to the ENFP because of their vision, enthusiasm and intuitive reasoning skills. Though these types share all four cognitive functions in common, they are arranged in a vastly different order and therefor manifest quite differently in each type.

What is functionally dominant in one type is tertiary in the other – for this reason, ESTJs and ENFPs get along best when each has developed their tertiary function. An ENFP with well-developed extroverted thinking can back up his or her lofty ideals with concrete actions, which impresses the ESTJ. On the flip side, the ESTJ with well-developed extroverted intuition can entertain (and follow through on) various theories and ideas, which delights the ENFP.

These types may struggle to connect via their auxiliary functions. The ENFP has auxiliary introverted feeling, which is inferior for the ESTJ. On the flip side, the ESTJ's auxiliary introverted sensing is inferior for the ENFP. The ENFP's disregard of tradition and the ESTJ's reluctance to open up emotionally may cause friction within the relationship. On the flip side, if both parties are invested in learning from the other and growing within the relationship, they can help one another develop their inferior functions and benefit greatly from one another.

Potential Challenges:

- The highly individualistic ENFP may see the ESTJ's constructive criticism as a personal attack or an attempt to control them, which can cause them to resent the ESTJ.

- The ESTJ may take the ENFP's resistance to their advice as a rejection, and consequently feel useless within the relationship.
- The ESTJ may require more stability from their lifestyle and their relationship than the ENFP is comfortable with.
- The ENFP may grow frustrated with the ESTJ's reluctance to open up emotionally. Conversely, the ESTJ may struggle to understand the ENFP's rapidly changing emotions.

How to make it work:

- Recognize the ways in which they show love – ESTJs are not particularly emotionally expressive but they express love by being undyingly loyal, diligent and committed to their partner.
- Express your needs clearly to the ESTJ – they may not intuitively understand your emotions but they respond well to being asked for help (I.e. If you are having a bad day and need some extra affection or help resolving a work problem, they will likely be more than happy to step in).
- When conflict arises, explain your reasoning to the ESTJ as concretely and logically as possible. If possible, give some action-oriented examples of how the issue could be resolved or avoided in the future.
- Appreciate that the ESTJ is attempting to help by

offering you their opinion – but don't be afraid to explain your point of view to them and affirm that you will be sticking with your own choice. Though they may not appreciate this initially, the ESTJ will ultimately respect you for your independence and follow-through.

ESTP

Cognitive Functions: Se – Ti – Fe – Ni

ESTPs are the direct, adventurous straight-shooters of the MBTI. ENFPs tend to be drawn to this type because of their cheerful demeanor, adventurous spirit and capable attitude. ESTPs tend to be drawn to ENFPs because of their independence, playfulness, and corresponding adventurous spirit. On the surface, these types seem quite similar. Below the surface, however, they share zero cognitive functions and process information in vastly different ways.

Though both types are adventurous and outgoing, for the ESTP this is driven by extroverted sensing – taking in the world exactly as it is and responding to it logically, via their auxiliary introverted thinking. On the flip side, the ENFP's extroverted intuition drives them to be more enticed by what could be than what is, and they make decisions about those ideas based on how they feel about them. Though both types are energized by new adventures, the ESTP is engaged in the physical rush of the immediate experience, whereas ENFPs enjoy adventuring for the purpose of adding new experiences to their repertoire for later reflection.

When it comes to decision-making, ESTPs are logical to a fault, whereas ENFPs turn to their feelings and subjective values to make decisions. This may cause friction within the relationship, as both parties may have trouble understanding the other's method of reasoning. While ESTPs and ENFPs share many surface similarities, they tend to experience great difficulty understanding one another when they become close. At worst, this causes the relationship to break down. At best, they learn form one another and find balance within their opposing sets of functions.

Potential Challenges:

- The ESTP may be confused or frustrated by the ENFP's tendency to discuss all the things they want to do (which the ESTP takes at face value) and then not follow through on them.
- The ENFP may feel as though they are lacking the deeper intellectual connection they tend to share with intuitive types.
- The ESTP may unintentionally hurt the ENFP's feelings with their direct communication style.
- The ENFP may grow frustrated by the ESTP's reluctance to open up emotionally – failing to

understand that the ESTP's tertiary extroverted feeling is oriented outward, into the world of action, rather than inward, into the world of introspection.

- Both parties may feel that the other is not accommodating enough of their whims, or nurturing enough to their needs. Some form of a power struggle may emerge, as both parties enjoy being the relationship's superhero.

How to make it work:

- Recognize the ways in which the ESTP is showing love – their tertiary extroverted feeling preference makes them want to play your 'superhero' and come to your aid whenever you're in need. They are showers, not tellers, but that does not mean their love is absent.
- Follow through on the plans you make with the ESTP –you will likely feel the most connected to each other when you're adventuring and having fun together.
- Validate and show admiration for the ESTP – emphasis what they bring to the relationship and what you appreciate them for.
- When conflict arises, be direct with the ESTP about which actions led to the problem. They don't care for sugarcoating issues or beating around the bush – they want to know exactly where the problem lies and what they can do to fix it.

INFP

Cognitive Functions: Fi-Ne-Si-Te

INFPs are the deep, compassionate healers of the MBTI. They share all four cognitive functions in common with the ENFP, in an only slightly different order, which allows these types to have a natural understanding of and appreciation for one another. The ENFP usually feels an immediate connection with the INFP and admires them for their patience, depth and moral conviction. The INFP in turn admires the ENFP for their strength, emotional intelligence and ability to put their visions into action. These types often possess similar worldviews and senses of humor, which makes them natural companions.

In terms of functions, what is dominant for the ENFP is auxiliary for the INFP and vice versa. The ENFP leads with extroverted intuition backed up by introverted feeling, whereas the INFP leads with introverted feeling, backed up by extroverted intuition. This means that the INFP's strengths lie in the emotional realm, whereas the ENFP's strengths lie in the realm of idea generation. So long as both parties are comfortable with their dominant function, they can help each other to learn more about and explore their auxiliary one. The ENFP can bring the INFP out of their head and help them to brainstorm new ideas when they are feeling stuck, whereas the INFP can ground the ENFP and help them to work through their emotions when the ENFP is having trouble processing them.

Just as the dominant and auxiliary functions for these types are reversed, so are their tertiary and inferior ones. Whereas the ENFP has tertiary extroverted thinking and inferior introverted sensing, the INFP has tertiary introverted sensing and inferior extroverted thinking. Though they may not learn from one another's tertiary or inferior functions, the opposing order may provide some degree of balance within the relationship – the ENFP is more adept than the INFP at putting concrete plans into motion, whereas the INFP is more adept than the ENFP at maintaining order and consistency.

These types share a natural sense of camaraderie and like-mindedness. The main challenge they may face in pursuing a close relationship is the lack of balance that their incredibly similar personalities provide.

Potential Challenges:

- The ENFP may fail to recognize the amount of alone time the INFP requires and take it personally when the INFP does not constantly want to spend time together. Conversely, the INFP may feel overwhelmed by the ENFP's high energy and brash personality.
- Because both parties have introverted decision-making functions, they may be slow to take

action or impose order on their external environment as a pair.

- Though both parties will likely feel a deep emotional bond, they may fail to effectively challenge one another, as their many similarities mean that they generally don't call on one another to think about things differently than they normally would.
- Because both parties are introverted feelers, feelings of competitiveness may develop between the two of them. Both want to be acknowledged for how unique they are, and if one threatens the other's uniqueness, things may turn petty.

How to make it work:

- As much as you appreciate your similarities, appreciate your differences too. Give each other validation for your individual strengths and acknowledge which unique traits each of you bring to the relationship.
- Respect the INFP's need for alone time and understand that it may take them slightly longer to warm up to new ideas than it takes you.
- Approach conflict kindly and openly. Explain to the INFP how a given situation made you feel using non-confrontational language, and then give them the chance to explain their own feelings.
- Be deliberate about structuring your external environment – both INFPs and ENFPs strive in structured environments but are not naturally adept

at creating them. Establish routines or schedules that suit both of your needs – this may pose a challenge initially but luckily, both types love a challenge!

ENFJ

Cognitive Functions: Fe – Ni – Se – Ti

ENFJs are the wise, nurturing teachers of the MBTI. ENFPs tend to find themselves drawn to this type because of their warmth, their depth and their similar system of values. ENFJs find themselves drawn to ENFPs because of their passion, their enthusiasm and their analytical nature. Despite being only one letter different from a dichotomous perspective, the ENFP and the ENFJ actually possess an entirely different set of cognitive functions.

Whereas the ENFP leads with their perceptive function, extroverted intuition, the ENFJ leads with their decision-making function, extroverted feeling. The ENFP's first function dwells in a perpetual state of intellectual chaos, whereas the ENFJ's first function seeks to help and harmonize with those around them.

The ENFJ backs up their feeling function with an intuitive one – in this case, introverted intuition. The ENFJ uses their introverted intuition to help them understand those around them on a deeper level and come up with ways to aid their loved ones in times of need. Despite being only one letter off, the combination of extroverted feeling and introverted intuition makes the ENFJ an incredibly different personality than the ENFP – they seek order and harmony whereas the ENFP seeks excitement and authenticity.

The ENFJ backs their dominant and auxiliary functions up with tertiary extroverted sensing and inferior introverted thinking. These functions give the ENFJ a keen appreciation for the aesthetic and the ability to seek out facts and objective truths within their otherwise emotion-ruled world. These functions once again differ from the ENFP's in terms of orientation and order.

These types often experience an initial connection and then are surprised to find how different they really are beneath the surface. However, all differences aside, when the ENFP and ENFJ take the time to truly understand and appreciate one another, they are more than capable of forming a meaningful, long-lasting bond.

Potential Challenges:

- The ENFJ may view the ENFP as selfish due to their preference for authenticity over harmonization.
- The ENFP may perceive the ENFJ's attempts to help or harmonize with them as an attempt to control them.
- These types may experience a mismatch of values on a deep level – both may feel that the other is emphasizing or focusing too much on unimportant issues and failing to acknowledge the important ones.

- Both parties may feel as though the other is refusing to listen to or learn from them.

How to make it work:

- Outwardly acknowledge that each party possesses a different set of traits and perceptions that the other can learn from.
- Practice understanding and taking interest in your opposing points of view, rather than passing judgment on them.
- When conflict arises, explain your feelings to the ENFJ in a non-confrontational manner and ask to hear theirs as well.
- Let the ENFJ know why and how much you appreciate them, on a regular basis. Tell them if a particular piece of advice they've given you worked for you. At the end of the day, the ENFJ wants to see you soar – they're happy if and when you are.

INFJ

Cognitive Functions: Ni – Fe – Ti – Se

INFJs are the deep, compassionate intellectuals of the MBTI. ENFPs find themselves drawn to this type because of their warmth, their intelligence and their grounding presence. The INFJs find themselves drawn to the ENFP because of their depth, their enthusiasm and their analytical nature. Despite sharing zero cognitive functions in common, these types are paradoxically among the best matches for each other. Because their functions are stacked in the same order, they offer a varied but intriguing perspective to each other – often taking different routes to arrive in the same place intellectually.

Just as the ENFP leads with their intuitive function (extroverted intuition), the INFJ leads with the inverse function, introverted intuition. Where the ENFP expands outward and connects abstract ideas, the INFJ narrows in and strips ideas down to their 'essence' or core. This provides the two with an intense intellectual connection, as both gain energy from analyzing new ideas and they tend to appreciate one another's opposite perspectives.

Both types also use feeling as an auxiliary function – introverted feeling for the ENFP and extroverted feeling for the INFJ. Though this type may experience some tension when it comes to their inverse feeling preferences (I.e. the INFJ over-accommodating for the ENFP), the ENFP generally appreciates the holistic approach the INFJ takes on philosophical issues due to their auxiliary extroverted feeling, whereas the INFJ usually appreciates the strong moral stances the ENFP reaches with their introverted feeling.

The tertiary and inferior functions of the INFJ (introverted thinking and extroverted sensing respectively) are once again stacked alongside the ENFP's in terms of order but oriented in the opposite direction. Once again, these functions can help each type appreciate the other – the INFJ may admire the drive the ENFP's extroverted thinking gives them and their ability to follow through on ideas via their introverted sensing, whereas the ENFP may admire the INFJ's ability to retain and analyze facts using their introverted thinking and the knack for the aesthetic that their extroverted sensing provides.

Potential Challenges:

- The INFJ may over-accommodate for the ENFP – potentially at the cost of compromising his or her own needs.
- The ENFP may be confused or hurt by the INFJ's need for alone time, since the INFJ acts so enthusiastic in social situations (but is, at the end of the day, still an introvert).
- The INFJ may be confused by the ENFP's (perceived) emotional inconsistencies and have trouble trusting them.
- Because their functions are all oriented in opposite directions, each party may have a difficult time understanding how the other arrived at a particular thought or decision.

How to make it work:

- Be patient with the INFJ's initial reluctance to open

up – they tend to approach relationships slowly, as their introverted intuition is constantly assessing whether or not they can trust newcomers.

- Ask the INFJ questions about themselves and the way their mind works – they will appreciate you taking the time to understand them.
- Respect the INFJ's need for introversion and be wary of their tendency to over-accommodate for loved ones. Check in with them regularly to ensure that their needs are being met.
- When conflict arises, be patient with the INFJ and ask to hear their side of the issue – they will appreciate you taking the time to see where they're coming from. Then, explain your side of the situation to them (without placing blame). Their introverted intuition will appreciate the opportunity to examine the issue from all angles.
- Reassure the INFJ (through words and actions alike) that despite your spontaneous nature and emotional ups and downs, you care about them and will be there for them consistently. Show them that they are a priority to you, because if the two of you are close, you are definitely a priority to them.

ENFP

Cognitive Functions: Ne – Fi – Te –Si

Having a relationship of any nature with someone of one's own type raises a particular set of challenges and joys. ENFPs find themselves drawn to other ENFPs because of their confidence and charm, as well as the ease of understanding that exists between them. These relationships tend to develop quickly and intensely – ENFPs usually feel as though they have a spiritual connection with one another and are often shocked to have found someone who understands them quite to the extent that the other ENFP does.

Of course, sharing all four cognitive functions in the same order is to blame for this immediate connection. Even when they are in disagreement with one another, each party is usually able to see the other's point of view and understand how they drew their conclusion. These types tend to feel particularly empathetic towards one another, as they've shared many of the same struggles and strengths over the course of their lives.

The health and success of a given relationship between two ENFPs is almost entirely dependent on the health of each individual. Between two confident, mature ENFPs, this pairing can be blissful and long lasting. Their shared extroverted intuition will keep things fresh and fun, whereas their introverted feeling function will keep them involved in a steady stream of validating and gushing over one another. Because they share many of the same emotional needs, they will be able to understand and respond to one another intuitively.

If, however, one of the ENFPs has unhealthy or under-developed introverted feeling, a sense of competition is likely to develop within the relationship. The ENFPs may fall into a pattern of consistently trying to one-up the other, in order to validate him or her self. This can lead to a quick deterioration of the relationship as resentment festers and pride takes precedence for both parties.

At the end of the day, the success of any ENFP-ENFP relationship is entirely dependent on the health and maturity of the ENFPs in question.

Potential Challenges:

- Because they share all four cognitive functions in the same order, the ENFPs may fail to challenge one another intellectually or practically the way someone with opposing functions might.
- A sense of competition may develop between two ENFPs if one or both of them has unhealthy or under-developed introverted feeling.
- In a partnership, the ENFPs may struggle to deal with day-to-day tasks such as paying the bills or maintaining an orderly household, as they introverted sensing is inferior for both of them.
- The relationship may lack emotional balance if the ENFPs find themselves to be too similar.

How to make it work:

- To avoid feelings of competition, nurture your own health and self-esteem and encourage the other ENFP to do the same.
- Appreciate and acknowledge your differences just as much as you appreciate and acknowledge your similarities.
- Find ways to challenge yourself intellectually and practically outside of the relationship.
- Don't assume that you always know what the other ENFP is thinking – remember that type does not holistically determine personality and that you still have to keep in touch with your partner's emotions and thoughts!

Part 7

Celebrating The ENFP

23

Embracing Your Identity As An ENFP

Life as an ENFP is no walk in the park. This type embodies a series of contradictions that can make life seem positively maddening at times. And yet, most ENFPs claim that they wouldn't trade their type in for the world. I surveyed all 16 personality types to see what exactly it is about ENFPs that makes them such an enticing, delightful type. Here's what some of them had to say.

Other Types Share What They Love About ENFPs

"I ADORE ENFPs! I love how chill they are, how they understand my deep emotions, and how welcoming they are to everyone. They can always see possibilities that I sometimes can't. Not to mention, they're SO FUN!"
–Bethany, INFP

"ENFPs manage to find something good in absolutely everyone they meet!"
–Libby, INFJ

"ENFPs draw me out and their thoughtful, fun-loving attitudes make them well-liked everywhere they go! The best thing about the ENFP is how special they make you feel when you get swept up into their exciting paths, leaving you wondering how you got in with such a cool person, but truly feeling like they really value your presence!"
–Sarah, INFP

"I love how they are both highly intelligent and very entertaining in social situations. They are able to keep up with me intellectually and get me to open up emotionally, and act friendly enough to me that I can hit it off with them, since as an introvert I have trouble reaching out to new people."
–Alan, INTJ

"I love how deep ENFPs are! And when you think you

have them figured out- nope! There is so much more!"
–Sabrina, ENFP

"I find joy in seeing ENFP's react to things. It seems to always be a genuine and incredibly animated reaction, it's amazing."
–Quincy, INTJ

"My two best friends are ENFPs! What I love about them is being able to talk about every subject or topic with an open mind and willing to learn new points of view. You never feel ashamed of your feelings, thoughts or opinions around ENFPs. It's pure love!"
–Ximena, ENFP

"They are honest and true to their core self which reflects in everything they do!"
–Katie, INFJ

"I love the ENFP badass spirit. They want to soak everything they can out of life. They explore, create, inspire, and love with their whole heart… and they want to share that with everyone! Also, their passion for growth and betterment for themselves and everyone else around them."
–Whitney, ENFP

"ENFPs can always get me off from my couch and motivate me to try and execute the things that I always kept planning to do."
–Kim, INFP

"I appreciate many things about ENFPs such as their zest for life and childlike sense of wonder and excitement about ideas! I also really appreciate their ability to draw me out of my shell to dream a little and help me to get better in touch with my emotions."
–Sara, ISTJ

"I love the way ENFPs make me get out of my comfort zone to explore new things!"
–Shannon, INTJ

"The ENFP enthusiasm is infectious and they are great people to talk through issues with. They can come up with five different solutions to a problem when I maybe would have only thought of two or three. In my experience they make awesome, supportive friends!"
–Kelli, ISFJ

"As a person who can be timid and reserved, ENFPs help me interact with people I wouldn't otherwise talk to. I now have many friends that I wouldn't if it were not for them!"
–Mandy, ISTJ

"My wife is an ENFP and I love so many things about her, but mostly I love that she makes me want to be a better person. She's compassionate, forgiving, and just so dang likable. Seriously, I don't think I've met a person with something bad to say about her! Her overall brightness and "goodness" is a perfect example of how I believe I should live

my life. I love what she is to and for me."
–Joel, INFJ

"They're among the few who can actually handle INTJs!"
–Mark, INTJ

"I love other ENFPs because they are hugs wrapped in
sunshine! Such warm folks! I love that we say the same thing
at the same time. I love that they love to hug. I love that they
are loud and fun and exuberant. I love that I start singing
anywhere and they will join me in singing and harmonizing.
I love that they appreciate diversity and variety in life. I love
that I can play silly games with them! Life without ENFPs
will be so dull!"
–Jamie, ENFP

ENFPs Share Their Favorite Part About Being An ENFP

"I love how optimistic I am! No matter what goes wrong, I
can find a way to get over it and move on with my life…
always onto bigger and better things. I know a lot of people
who get stuck in their problems for such a long time but
that's definitely not me. I see a thousand ways around
everything!"
-Tracey, 49

"This might sound corny but I think that being an ENFP is such a magical thing. We are so full of love – I sometimes feel like I'm going to burst because my heart is so full! We just see so much good in everything and everyone around us... the world needs more ENFPs!"
-Angie, 41

"I love how comfortable I can make people feel, even people I barely know or just met!"
-Sara, 16

"What I love about myself as an ENFP is that I'm constantly trying to grow and be a better person and that I am so resilient. I've suffered a lot of pretty bad experiences in my life but I still think the world is promising and that people are essentially good."
-Kaitlyn, 43

"I like that I am confident, capable and a little bit crazy. I honestly even like the downsides of being an ENFP, like being a bit manipulative or sneaky. Those traits can be useful."
-Heather, 19

"I like that I care so much about other people. Even if it means I get hurt sometimes, I wouldn't trade being able to feel and love this deeply."
-Landon, 24

"I love my ENFP charm!"
-Jacob, 24

"I love being able to switch from silly and playful to serious and contemplative. I love the sense of joy and love we bring to our lives and to the lives of others! Even the bad has meaning to us and I think that's more important than other people understand."
–Dylan, 22

"We have the ability to see the good in every person, in every situation – even the downright awful – we turn it around and shine some light on it. We have the ability soldier on, no matter how heartbroken or upset or hard done by we are… we get through it with our inner strength and the eternal promise of a better tomorrow. Our endless optimism ensures this. I think that's why I am the person I am today, still soldiering on, still living life as best I can!"
–Caz, 25

"I like that I can lead a group, sit in solitude for days, think far ahead, improvise, be a huge ball of energy, calm down others when they're stressed, be a mushball, be tough and decisive, create new opportunities for myself, adapt to the world around me… I defy so many stereotypes and I like it that way!"
–Amber, 30

"What's NOT to love about being an ENFP? Life is an

adventure!"
–Jess, 36

"I like getting irrationally excited over everything... like the smell of springtime or a new flavor of tea. Some people don't understand my enthusiasm about strange little things but it's honestly one of my favorite parts of being an ENFP!"
–Erica, 27

"ENFPs are so full of life! It's like we never hit rock bottom because there's always another great idea to distract ourselves with. We CRUSH every challenge that gets in our way!"
–Mackenzie, 21

"Two words: Endless optimism."
–Alex, 34

"I used to hate being misunderstood by others but I've grown to love it as I age. People think you're bubbly and then you hit them with your intelligence. People think you're flakey and then you hit them with your determination. People think you're selfish and then you hit them with your massive well of compassion and understanding. Proving people wrong is fun and ENFPs do it ALL the time!"
–Carl, 44

"Even on the bad days, life is a big, passionate adventure, filled with people to love and opportunities to explore! Would being more down-to-earth or more organized be cool? Maybe. But not if I had to lose my energy and creativity

and confidence!”
–Aimee, 23

“I LIKE THAT LIFE IS MESSY! There, I said it. I know most people want to walk down a perfectly straight path in life but I don't. I like the twists and turns. I like not knowing what's coming next. My life may not seem normal to those around me but I don't care. A normal life would be boring. And I hate being bored.”
–Duncan, 41

About the Author

Heidi Priebe graduated from the University of Guelph, Ontario with a degree in Psychology and the firm ambition to prove her skeptical professors wrong about the Myers-Briggs Type Indicator. When she's not blogging about the sixteen types, Heidi enjoys traveling for long periods of time as a means of avoiding her problems. She is a textbook Type 7 ENFP. This is her first book.

Works Cited

Quenk, Naomi L. *Was That Really Me?: How Everyday Stress Brings out Our Hidden Personality.* Palo Alto, CA: Davies-Black Pub., 2002. Print.

Riso, Don Richard, and Russ Hudson. *The Wisdom Of The Enneagram.* New York: Bantam, 1997. Print.

"The Myers & Briggs Foundation – Lifelong Type Development." *The Myers & Briggs Foundation – Lifelong Type Development.* Web. 11 Sept. 2015

Thought Catalog, it's a website.
www.thoughtcatalog.com

Social
facebook.com/thoughtcatalog
twitter.com/thoughtcatalog
tumblr.com/thoughtcatalog
instagram.com/thoughtcatalog

Corporate
www.thought.is

Printed in Great Britain
by Amazon